Work & Live Anywhere:

Peru Unplugged

By Tara Richter-Hatzilias

Copyright © 2025 Tara Richter-Hatzilias

All rights reserved. In accordance with U.S. Copyright Act of 1976, the scanning, uploading, and electronic sharing of any part of this book without permission of the publisher constitute unlawful piracy and theft of the author's intellectual property. No part of this book may be reproduced in any form by any electronic or mechanical means (including photocopying, recording or information storage and retrieval) without permission in writing from the author or publisher. Thank you for your support of the author's rights.

Published by Richter Publishing LLC www.richterpublishing.com

Book Cover Design: Tara Richter

Editors: Sofia Diaz-Ojeda, Adriana Hartman, Sophia Gerneck, Lux Figueroa & Heather Pickert

Photos: By Tara Richter-Hatzilias unless other credit has been specified

ISBN-13: 978-1-954094-67-3

DISCLAIMER

This book is designed to provide information on working and living in Peru only. This information is provided and sold with the knowledge that the publisher and author do not offer any legal or medical advice. In the case of a need for any such expertise consult with the appropriate professional. This book does not contain all information available on the subject. This book has not been created to be specific to any individual people or organization's situation or needs. Reasonable efforts have been made to make this book as accurate as possible. However, there may be typographical and or content errors. Therefore, this book should serve only as a general guide. This book contains information that might be dated or erroneous and is intended only to educate and entertain. The author and publisher shall have no liability or responsibility to any person or entity regarding any loss or damage incurred, or alleged to have incurred, directly or indirectly, by the information contained in this book or as a result of anyone acting or failing to act upon the information in this book. You hereby agree never to sue and to hold the author and publisher harmless from any and all claims arising out of the information contained in this book. You hereby agree to be bound by this disclaimer, covenant not to sue and release. There may be links in this book to various sites. While the author and publisher take no responsibility for any virus or technical issues that could be caused by such links, the business practices of these companies and or the performance of any product or service, the author or publisher has used the product or service and makes a recommendation in good faith based on that experience. All characters appearing in this work are fictitious. Any resemblance to real persons, living or dead, is purely coincidental. The opinions and stories in this book are the views of the author and not those of the publisher.

"The journey of a thousand miles begins with a single step."

— *Lao Tzu*

DEDICATION

I dedicate this book to all the people who have wanderlust in their souls. To the people who have a strong desire or impulse to travel and explore the world. Who constantly have a deep yearning for adventure, new experiences, and discovering different cultures and places. You seek the joy that comes from experiencing the unfamiliar. Along with the personal growth from taking the courage to live outside your comfort zone. In these current political climates, we need more people who are willing to go and explore other parts of the globe to understand how the rest of the world lives. If we can walk a mile in someone else's shoes, maybe just maybe, the world could become a better place.

"The world is a book, and those who do not travel read only one page."

— *Saint Augustine*

"Once a year, go someplace you've never been before."

— *Dalai Lama*

Table of Contents

Chapter 1 Visas 1

Chapter 2 What to Pack 8

Chapter 3 When to Go 22

Chapter 4 Where to Stay...25

Chapter 5 Scams in Peru 37

Chapter 7 Protests in Peru & Political Unrest 59

Chapter 8 Food..69

Chapter 9 Machu Picchu 76

Chapter 10 Working Remotely..90

Chapter 11 Rainbow Mountain 101

Chapter 12 Sand Dunes & Sea Lions 104

Chapter 13 Manicures & Pedicures in Peru 118

Chapter 14 Travel Insurance and Hurricanes.................124

Chapter 15 Final Thoughts 128

About the Author 130

"Not all those who wander are lost."

— *J.R.R. Tolkien*

ACKNOWLEDGMENTS

I would like to extend my heartfelt thanks to the incredible interns at the USF English Dept who supported me throughout the editing process of this book. Your sharp eyes, thoughtful feedback, and unwavering dedication brought fresh perspective and clarity to these pages. Each of you contributed not only your time and talent, but also your passion for storytelling and commitment to excellence. I am truly grateful for your hard work, your patience through every revision, and the energy you brought to this project. This book is stronger because of you—and I couldn't have done it without your help.

To my husband—thank you for always supporting my love of travel, even when the plans are wild, the bags are overpacked, and the destinations are halfway across the world (or just slightly off the beaten path). Your enthusiasm, humor, and patience make every adventure more fun, every mishap more bearable, and every memory infinitely better. Whether we're exploring new cities, getting lost in foreign streets, or just soaking in the moment with friends, I wouldn't want to do it with anyone else. Here's to all the places we've been, and all the crazy, beautiful ones still waiting for us.

INTRODUCTION

Peru stands as a beacon of history, culture, and natural beauty in South America, attracting travelers from all corners of the globe. This guide aims to provide you with an essential overview of what makes Peru an unforgettable destination, including its key attractions and practical tips. From ancient Incan ruins to colonial architecture, Peru is a country rich in history and archaeological splendor. No visit to Peru is complete without witnessing the awe-inspiring sight of Machu Picchu. Nestled high in the Andes Mountains, this 15th-century Incan citadel is a UNESCO World Heritage Site and one of the New Seven Wonders of the World. Whether you hike the iconic Inca Trail or take the train, the majestic beauty and historical significance of Machu Picchu are undeniable. Once the capital of the Incan Empire, Cusco serves as the gateway to Machu Picchu and a hub for exploring Peru's rich history. Its well-preserved colonial architecture blends seamlessly with Incan sites, such as Sacsayhuamán and Qorikancha, offering a unique glimpse into Peru's past.

Beyond its historical attractions, Peru's diverse landscapes, ranging from Amazon rainforests to Lake Titicaca, make it a country of unparalleled natural beauty. The Peruvian Amazon covers about 60% of the country, offering adventurers the chance to explore one of the world's most biodiverse areas. Meanwhile, Lake Titicaca, the world's highest navigable lake, provides stunning views and a chance to visit the unique floating islands of Uros.

The fusion of Indigenous, Spanish, African, and Asian influences has created a rich cultural tapestry and one of the world's most celebrated cuisines. From enjoying ceviche in Lima to savoring Andean delicacies in Cusco, the culinary experiences in Peru are as diverse as its heritage.

Traveling to Peru offers an invaluable opportunity to explore a land where the past and present coexist harmoniously. By engaging with its history, indulging in its diverse cuisines, and experiencing its unique landscapes, visitors will find themselves enchanted by Peru's rich cultural heritage and natural beauty. This makes Peru the perfect place for digital nomads.

After 2020, remote work has increased tenfold. The rise of digital nomadism after COVID-19 can be attributed to several factors:

1. **Remote Work Adoption**: The pandemic forced many companies to adopt remote work policies. As a result, employees discovered the feasibility of working from anywhere, leading to a shift in mindset about where work can be performed.
2. **Flexible Work Options**: Organizations began to offer more flexible work arrangements, allowing employees to live where they choose, rather than being tied to a traditional office setting.
3. **Desire for Lifestyle Change**: The pandemic prompted many individuals to reassess their life priorities. People sought new experiences, freedom, and a better work-life balance, motivating them to explore life as digital nomads.
4. **Advancements in Technology**: Technology facilitated seamless communication and collaboration across distances. With reliable internet and digital tools, working remotely became more effective and efficient.

5. **Increased Interest in Travel**: After extended periods of lockdown, many people were eager to travel again. The combination of remote work and the desire to explore new places spurred the digital nomad trend.
6. **Community and Resources**: The growth of online communities and resources catering to digital nomads has made it easier for newcomers to find support, meet others, and access information about living and working abroad.

Overall, the combination of changing workplace dynamics, personal aspirations, and technological advancements has led to an increase in the digital nomad lifestyle post-COVID.

In this book, we will cover multiple topics to help you on your nomadic journey, so you too can work and live the life you have always wanted! What you will learn:

1. What to pack
2. Where to stay
3. What times of the year to go
4. What to eat
5. Where to work remotely
6. How to get to popular destinations like Machu Picchu
7. And of course, what not to do & how to avoid scams

This is based on my experience after staying in Peru for the entire month in September 2022. I decided for my 45th birthday I was going to finally accomplish the bucket list item of hiking the massive mountain, Machu Picchu. My travel buddy Jeff and I decided, why not just stay the entire month? We can both work remotely, so the journey began!

Chapter 1 Visas

For United States citizens traveling to Peru for tourism or business purposes, you do not need a visa if your stay is 90 days or less. You'll only need:

- **A valid passport (must be valid for at least 6 months beyond your entry date).** This is an important thing to note when traveling to any foreign country, and Peru is no exception! A friend of mine traveled to Greece when she was young, and her passport was set to expire within that 6-month window. So when she arrived in Greece, she wasn't allowed into the country. She lost hotel bookings, excursions, and multiple other things besides having to pivot and book plane tickets to another country that would allow them entry. Don't get stuck in her shoes!
- **Proof of onward or return travel (sometimes requested by airlines or immigration).** Another travel secret I was naïve about until country hopping in Asia. I was almost not allowed on the plane to Vietnam because I didn't have a return flight out of Vietnam. Since I was with a travel group, I was supposed to only book my flight from

the U.S. to Hanoi, then they booked all of our transportation after that. Well, the airlines and Vietnam want to know that I am planning on *leaving* their country and not moving there without proper documentation. Delta almost made me book a return flight even though I didn't need one. It was a shock and something I wasn't prepared for. I wish the travel company would have given us our flight info to Thailand before we left the States; that would have been really nice! However, when we did a month in Europe, I was prepared for this and had all of our travel docs ready. We did have a return flight this time, so it wasn't an issue. This is also why I print everything out just in case, so I can show proof of our travel plans to anyone who needs to see them right away, even when I don't have a Wi-Fi connection. For example, when arriving in Japan, I was held up in customs because the customs agents wanted the address of where I was going to stay, and there was zero WIFI in the building. I had to text the travel group for our address, which prolongated the whole experience. I was then held up again when security thought our group had drugs on us, because one of our travel mates had just gotten a sleeve tat on his arm. But that is a story for another time.

In Peru, we were only staying for 30 days, so we did not have to do anything prior to traveling. Different countries, though, have different policies. Like for Vietnam, I applied for a visa prior to going, so I already had my papers when I arrived. It cost me $30 which I didn't think was expensive. You could have received a visa on arrival, however, after traveling 36 hours, I didn't want any hiccups at customs.

Visas For Longer Stays

If you're planning to stay longer than 90 days, or traveling for purposes other than tourism or business (e.g., work, study, or residency), you'll need to apply for the appropriate visa through the Peruvian Consulate. These are the types of visas you can get for staying in Peru. This is a general breakdown of visas for U.S. Citizens. Always double check for the most accurate, up-to-date information.

Tourist Visa Extension

- If you enter as a tourist, you can **request an extension** (online or at immigration offices) for up to **183 days** in total.
- **No work is allowed** on this visa. Yet digital nomad, online work is ok, if you do it discreetly.

Business Visa

- For **work-related activities** (e.g., meetings, conferences), valid for **up to 183 days**.
- Does not permit full-time employment in Peru.
- Requires an invitation letter from a Peruvian company.

Work Visa

- For **long-term employment** in Peru.
- Requires a **job contract** with a Peruvian company and approval from the labor ministry.
- Typically valid for **1 year,** renewable.

Student Visa

- For individuals enrolled in **Peruvian educational institutions.**
- Requires proof of enrollment and financial support.
- Valid for **1 year**, renewable.

Family Visa

- For **family reunification** (spouse, children, or parents of a Peruvian citizen or resident).
- Valid for **1 year**, renewable.
- Allows you to work legally.

Rentista Visa (Retirement or Passive Income)

- For individuals with **stable, passive income** (e.g., pension or rental income).
- Requires proof of **$1,000+ monthly income**.
- Grants **indefinite residency** with no work allowed.

Investor Visa

- For individuals investing at least **$150,000 USD** in a Peruvian business.
- Valid for **1 year**, renewable.
- Allows you to **own and run a business**.

Peru at this time does not offer a digital nomad visa. However, many other countries understand the benefit of having digital nomads in their countries and do offer them. To have people working, living, and spending money to help boost your local economy while not taking away jobs, I think, is a win-win for any nation. Here is a breakdown of places that have programs for digital nomads (again this info can change at any time.)

Latin America & Caribbean

1. 🇨🇷 **Costa Rica – Rentista Visa**
    - Income requirement: **$3,000/month** or $60,000 in savings.
    - Valid for **2 years,** renewable.
    - Tax-free income.
2. 🇧🇷 **Brazil – Digital Nomad Visa**
    - Income requirement: **$1,500/month** or $18,000 in savings.
    - Valid for **1 year,** renewable.
    - No local taxes on foreign income.
3. 🇨🇴 **Colombia – Digital Nomad Visa**
    - Income requirement: **$900/month**.
    - Valid for **2 years**.
    - Includes access to healthcare system.
4. 🇩🇴 **Dominican Republic – Remote Work Visa**
    - Income requirement: **$1,500/month.**
    - Valid for **1 year,** renewable.
    - Tax-free foreign income.

Europe

1. 🇵🇹 **Portugal – D7 or Digital Nomad Visa**
    - Income requirement: **€3,280/month**.
    - Valid for **1 year,** renewable.
    - Tax benefits under NHR (Non-Habitual Residency) program.
2. 🇪🇸 **Spain – Digital Nomad Visa**

- Income requirement: **€2,600/month**.
- Valid for **1 year**, renewable up to **5 years**.
- 15-24% tax on income.
3. 🇬🇪 **Georgia – Remotely from Georgia Program**
    - Income requirement: **$2,000/month**.
    - Valid for **1 year**.
    - Tax-free if staying less than 183 days.

Asia & Oceania

1. 🇮🇩 **Bali, Indonesia – Second Home Visa**
    - Income requirement: **$2,000/month**.
    - Valid for **5 or 10 years**.
    - Tax-free, foreign income.
2. 🇲🇾 **Malaysia – DE Rantau Nomad Visa**
    - Income requirement: **$24,000/year**.
    - Valid for **1 year**, renewable.
    - No local tax on foreign income.

It's surprising that Thailand doesn't have a nomad visa, considering Chiang Mai is home to the largest expat community in the world. However, when I lived there for two months back in 2019, expats were basically working the system. A basic tourist visa on arrival is 60 days, which you can then extend by 30 days, meaning you will be legally allowed to stay for 90 days. Then, there were companies that would do border crossings into Laos. They would take a busload of people whose visas were expiring, drive them over the border, and then come right back to stamp their passports because they got so many renewals in a year. You could only do so many by land and so many by air.

I personally thought it was more fun country hopping. This is why we stayed 30 days, then were off to the next place, while I was with my travel group in Asia because most countries give you a free 30-day visa upon arrival. Spend a month, do, see, and eat everything! Then a few days before it's up, book a plane ticket to the next adventure. It's like The Amazing Race. Each month you are learning a new language, new customs, new ways to cross the street. It is literally the best high I have ever had in my life. I will go into all the details of country hopping in Asia in my next book!

COVID Vaccines

When we were in Peru back in 2022, you had to have two COVID-19 vaccinations in order to get into the country. However, you didn't need a negative test, just the card. You had to have your card on you or a digital version of it at all times. They were a lot stricter with that than in the U.S. For example, going into some public establishments, we had to show our vaccination cards. It got to the point where I actually put my card as the photo on the background pic on my iPhone because I didn't want to lose my actual card. They said you also needed these to enter Machu Picchu, but they never asked for it at the gate. But this was back in 2022. A quick search on Google in 2025 states that they do not require this anymore. The CDC recommends vaccinations for various diseases, including yellow fever, hepatitis A, typhoid, and polio, depending on your travel plans and destination in Peru. But always check current info prior to traveling.

Chapter 2 What to Pack

Depending on what time of year you're going to Peru, this list is what I recommend to pack for the wintertime. Miraflores area is going to be chilly, windy, and sometimes a little rainy. It is often nice during the day when the sun is out. However, it is certainly chillier at night. When the sun is down, I definitely recommend dressing in layers.

1. **Shoes:** Tennis shoes or good walking shoes. The streets are paved well, but at times are uneven. I do not recommend flip-flops or heels. Being a Florida girl, I wear my flip-flops every day. But when traveling, I usually bring tennis shoes, a good pair of hiking shoes, and maybe one pair of flip-flops. Pack good ones, like Sketchers, that are comfortable for walking distances. Make sure to get a decent pair of hiking boots if you plan on hiking as well. I invested in a nice pair of hiking boots that are waterproof. Prioritize comfort over all else! I had to get men's Columbia boots, because my feet are too big for women's to fit comfortably. Figure out what you will need to be comfortable and invest in it.

Know that when you are out there hiking for ten-some hours, you will really need comfort.

2. **Socks:** Pack double the socks you think you're going to need. I didn't pack enough of them, and I had to buy more. For hiking days, I really like merino wool socks. They are much better than just regular cotton ones because they will absorb sweat, and your feet will not smell like a wet dog after a long day's hike. They are pricey, sure, but so worth it.

3. **Leggings:** I liked wearing leggings for nighttime because with the winds (and it does get windy at night, especially on the coast) it gets chilly, so the leggings are nice and keep your legs warm. Plus, I like leggings that have pockets because I can put my cell phone in them. We never had any problems with pick pocketing, but it can happen. That's why I like the leggings with pockets because you would have to basically feel up my thigh to get my cell phone. And they would get punched in the face before that happened.

4. **Quick-Dry Shirts:** I love the quick-dry material in everything possible. Not only because it's breathable during the day when it gets hot out during peak times, but also because the clothes dry faster, too. If you ever do laundry in another country, most countries do not have dryers. They have drying racks to hang your clothes on so they can air-dry. So, if you have cotton shirts, it's going to take much longer to dry versus the quick-dry material. Plus, they don't wrinkle in your suitcase.

5. **Tennis Skirts:** This is a life hack my girlfriends and I have been using for years in Florida. I LOVE tennis skirts, yet I don't play tennis. They are super cute and have the little

shorts underneath them. They are stretchy, comfortable, and made of the quick-dry material. They are everything you need during the heat in the Florida summertime, or anywhere else, when you are out walking around for hours during the day and still want to look cute and not get the chafing on your thighs.

6. **Sunscreen:** Buy sunscreen at home. It's really expensive in Peru. I'm not sure why, but every time I travel outside the United States, sunscreen is always super expensive. However, I didn't need too much other than when we did one trip to the Sand Dunes where it was really sunny. Most of the time it was cool, and I didn't really need it. But the tiny bottle I did buy was like a small travel size for $30.

7. **Medicine:** Definitely pack any medicine you need or *might* need. Even over-the-counter stuff like Sudafed. They do not have Sudafed in other countries or things like Flonase—which I didn't pack and it ended up being a big problem for me because I had a bad allergy attack. When I was there, I needed something to treat the attack, and I didn't know how to describe it to the pharmacist. I did, however, finally find a website that identified alternatives for specific medicine in other countries. It is called pillintrip.com. That actually helped more than talking to the pharmacist did. First, look up the medicine you want, then find the comparable medication on the website, and then show that to the pharmacist. I finally got something similar to what I needed, and it really helped me out.

8. **Thermometers**: I always think it's good to travel with a cheap thermometer. You never know when you or someone else is going to get sick, especially now with

COVID running rampant. If you get a cold, you'd want to know if it's just that or something more. I bought one from the dollar store in the United States before I went to Asia back in April 2019. That $1 thermometer served me well for five years. I'm so glad I had it then, because in Japan I got walking pneumonia, and my temperature was up to one hundred and three degrees. I was burning up. I'm so glad I had to keep track of my temperature because if it didn't go down, I would have gone to the hospital. Hospitals in Japan are really expensive, and I didn't buy travel health insurance, either. You cannot just get amoxicillin over the counter in Japan like you can in Vietnam, Thailand, or Greece. (By the way, you can get this in Thailand for about $3 a two-pack, which is an entire round). Thankfully, my travel mate had some and gave me three pills, which were enough to break my fever and make me well enough to travel back to Thailand in two days. So, I waited until I got back there, bought the amoxicillin over the counter for $3, and was back to normal. Because of my Japan experience, I always buy amoxicillin when traveling, just to keep on me in case someone gets sick. Better to be safe than sorry.

9. **Small Portable Fans:** These are a game changer. I bought some small camping fans on Amazon, that claimed they had a battery life of forty hours, for some outside vendor events in Florida. These little bad boys are small but put off an amazing breeze. I literally take them with me everywhere! Doesn't matter if I am going to a cold climate destination or a warm weather one. (When I sleep, I like to have air movement—I cannot stand stale air). And if it's hot, well, these little guys are small enough to put in your backpack or purse. The batteries really do last forty hours long. I would use them all day long and then charge them at night.

As a bonus, the fans have an LED light, so you can also use them as a nightlight, which comes in handy. The lighting situation in a lot of the Airbnbs were a tad confusing. If I got up in the middle of the night to use the bathroom, I didn't want to turn on all the lights or fumble around trying to figure out which light switch was what. Instead, I would just use the fan. Here is the link to Amazon. I highly recommend these:

https://www.amazon.com/dp/B07RZC56WX/
REENUO 5000mAh Camping Fan with LED Lights, 40 Hours Max Working Time Tent Fan with Hanging Hook, Rechargeable Battery.

10. **Packing Cubes:** I love packing cubes. I learned this from my travel mates in Asia. It really helps to keep you organized when traveling, so you can only pull out what you need and not have a big mess in your suitcase. I like to organize them by putting all shirts in one cube, leggings in another, socks and underwear in another, etc. They even come with shoe bags and dirty laundry bags.

11. **Soles:** Bring money with you. Get some local currency before you leave because if you need to get a ride from the airport, then you'd better have cash on you. Some taxis take card payments, some don't. A lot of other countries, especially Third World ones, are cash based and don't use cards. It's always good sense to have some local currency on you because not all countries will accept your currency.

I travel to Mexico a lot and was used to them just always accepting USD, so when I went to Vietnam, I just naively assumed they would too. I didn't get Vietnamese Dong before I went there—big mistake! Not only would they not accept my USD, most cafes wouldn't accept any cards, either. I barely ate the first three days of my trip; it was a tough lesson being in a foreign country with no cash and no cards that worked.

12. **Passports:** Obviously, you need your passport with you. However, make sure you check your expiration date. Peru, along with many other countries, will not let you in the country if your passport expires within six months of your entry. So, check your passport, and renew it in time if you're close to the deadline.

13. **Copies of Passport & Other Documents:** I'm a tad over-organized, but when it comes to international travel, I do not want to lose anything, especially something as important as a passport, flight information, or hotel bookings. So, what I do is, before traveling, I scan and print copies of all our important paperwork. Passports, flight information, hotel confirmations, credit cards we are carrying (in case we get robbed), American driver's license, driving directions to hotels, really anything that is important. I keep it on my clipboard in my backpack, and I also back it up to the cloud in case I lose the hard copies. This also comes in handy because you do not always have Wi-Fi in other countries. So, when we are in a cab and the driver wants the address to our hotel, I just hand them the sheet of paper with the address on it. Addresses in other countries can look very different than American addresses, and everyone who travels internationally can relate to

struggling to pronounce the names of streets sometimes. It's easier for the driver to see it in black and white. At the hotel, I can pull out my clipboard, flip through all our reservations, and see the time frame in which we need to check out. It's nice to have everything organized in one place that doesn't require Wi-Fi to access the information. This has saved my ass multiple times. Once, when we went to visit the Mayan ruins in Tulum, Mexico from a cruise ship excursion, our tour guide abandoned us. We were almost left behind in Playa Del Carman, and our guide never came back for us! Thankfully, another tour guide led us back to our ferry just in the nick of time; but even if we had ended up stranded in Mexico, it would've been fine, because we had those hard copies of our passports and other vital documents to book plane tickets back to Florida.

14. **Travel Jewelry:** After extensively globetrotting for now half of my life to many different parts of the world, some things that you particularly want to pay attention to, depending upon what part of the world you're in, is the type of jewelry you bring with you. If you're traveling to a First World country, this generally isn't a problem, but you still want to be smart and, of course, keep your street smarts about you. For instance, even in NYC, I almost got my entire suitcase stolen the first night trying to get into my Airbnb because I wasn't paying attention. My travel buddy, Jeff, and I were trying to get the lock open to get the key out. It was one of the realtor lock boxes attached to a fence outside on the street, and he couldn't get it open. Since I also have a real-estate license (yes, I have so much spare time to do that as well) and more experience with these contraptions, I walked two feet away from my suitcase to help. Instead of pulling it along with me, I bent

down to help him unlock the mechanism. Within those two minutes of not keeping an eye on my suitcase, a man walked over and stated out loud, "Oh, here's my suitcase—I've been looking all over for it." I jumped up and screamed back, "No, that's mine!" and grabbed it out of his hands. Maybe he was teaching me a lesson for being so naïve, thinking I could leave it unattended and not with my arm wrapped around it for just a few seconds on the streets of New York. I'm not from the big city, so I don't think about those things. But I do when I'm in a Third World country. Maybe it's because I've spent more time in Third World countries than I have in big cities.

I have honestly not had expensive jewelry most of my life. However, even when I was younger traveling to Third World countries, I have always made a point of not wearing anything expensive. Not even name brand shoes. But now that I have an expensive diamond ring, I want to keep it, and myself, safe. When we are from First World countries, we don't think twice about going outside with a $20,000 diamond ring on our fingers because we know we are going to be safe. But in a Third World country, that could possibly buy someone a house. So, we need to put ourselves in their shoes, literally, and have common sense before we go over to their world to explore, so we don't end up as a statistic.

My father had a catamaran built in South Africa many years ago because it was much cheaper to do so there. It took a lot longer than expected to get done because they took lots of siestas during the workday. He flew over there with my brother Troy, and they ended up living in Durban, South Africa for almost two months while the boat finished being built. While they were there, they ended up getting a reputation as two White, rich men in the area.

Not necessarily a good thing you want locals to know. But my dad likes to flaunt his wealth, and everything's very cheap there, too. So, at night, he would take out the boat workers for dinner and drinks as his way of saying thank you and pay for everything. However, it a so draws a lot of attention. Now, my brother is a big guy, standing at six feet tall. Though he's tall, he's still the nicest guy on the planet and would never hurt a fly. My dad is five foot nine, not as tall as him. Of course, they went over there in their expensive name brand shoes and wearing nice watches. Normally, they would walk the streets together, but one day, my father went out by himself. That was a mistake. He turned down an alleyway where he got jumped by two local men. They swung a knife at his heart and tried to murder him for his watch, shoes, and wallet. They didn't just ask for his stuff; they went straight for his heart. They didn't care. Thankfully, he had quick reaction time and some training in Jiu-jitsu; he grabbed the knife, so it didn't stab him, but it did cut off the top of his thumb. He struggled with them long enough that they ran off. Then, a local woman came to his rescue. She called an ambulance and rode with him to make sure the paramedics took him to the right hospital where they wouldn't rip him off for being a tourist and scam him in order to sew his thumb back on.

Even before this incident, I always dressed down in Third World countries. No name brands, basic shirt with no logos, basic shoes, knapsacks for purses, and no jewelry. You do not want to make yourself a target. These people tried to murder my dad for his shoes. It's not worth it. You should not be a flashy American in Third World countries. Well, you could, but you would also pay the price.

When I was in Egypt visiting the pyramids of Giza with my mother back in 2009, I was wearing my "plain outfit" with nothing sparkly at all. We were in front of the iconic pyramids taking pictures. Men on camels kept coming up to us, wanting to take us on camel rides, and we kept declining them. Yet, this one Egyptian man was really persistent and kept following me. He reached out, grabbed my arm, and pulled me towards him on the camel. I pulled back, and he swiped his hands over mine, trying to steal any rings or jewelry I had on me. Thankfully, I never wore anything when

traveling, so he got nothing from me. But it was a super creepy experience I will never forget.

Even knowing this, I still wore my diamond ring traveling to Peru, and as soon as I got there, I remembered, *I don't wear jewelry when traveling*. I honestly forgot. I felt stupid wearing my big-ass, shiny, diamond ring because NOBODY was wearing anything even close to it, and it just drew attention to me. Not to mention, you cannot haggle with street vendors wearing that. They don't believe you don't have money wearing that on your finger. Which brings me to the point: you can either wear no jewelry, or you can make imitations of your actual jewelry pieces for travel purposes. After the first few days in Peru, I hid my ring safely out of site and didn't wear it for the rest of the trip. Yet, I still wanted to have a ring on my finger, so I thought we needed to make a travel ring. Something that isn't as flashy, smaller maybe even with cubic zirconia, so if I lose it, it's not that big of a deal. I still wanted to show the world that I'm married without the risk of being mugged or murdered in a Third World country.

15. **Outlets in Peru:** Peru uses the same two-pronged, flat plugs as the ones in the United States. I didn't need a converter for anything I was using which basically was my iPhone, iWatch, and laptop. I was only plugging in bricks to charge everything, which was totally fine. The standard voltage in Peru is 220V, so you should come with a converter for 110-volt devices. Thankfully, if you are using Apple devices, Apple's iPhone chargers work with voltage anywhere in the world—110V, 115V, 120V, 220V, 230V, 240V, and whatever else you might find. Since I was using all Apple products, I didn't have an issue. The little brick will do the converting for you. However, if you have, say, a blow-dryer or flat iron,

you will need a converter. Otherwise, you might see smoke when plugging it in.

16. **Extended Monitors:** Since I am running my publishing house, when I am working remotely, it's hard for me to do design work in Photoshop on my small Mac screen. I like having a portable extended monitor with me. I got one on Amazon for $100, and it is awesome. You can get a dual monitor if you need even more space. One of my travel friends had that setup when we were country-hopping in Asia. I didn't want too much in my backpack weighing me down, so I opted for just one. It can go vertical or horizontal, which is cool. The only thing is that it has to be plugged into the power supply of your Mac to work, so it really drains your battery life. The only way for it to work is to be set up at a desk with your extensions plugged in for extra cords, plug the monitor in, and then hook it all into a power supply. Otherwise, your computer will die in about an hour. That is the only downside.

KEFEYA

Visit the Store   4.6 ★★★★½ (3,933)

Laptop Screen Extender, 14" FHD 1080P IPS Laptop Monitor Extender Dual Screen, Portable Monitor for Laptops 13-17" with USB-C/HDMI Port, Plug n Play for Windows/Mac/Android/Switch/PS5

Amazon's Choice

◊ 3 sustainability features ∨

6K+ bought in past month

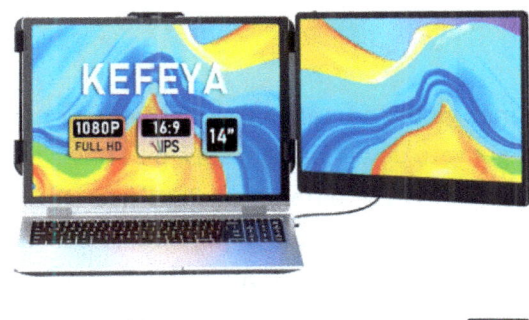

Chapter 3 When to Go

Deciding when to go to Peru can make or break your trip. Knowing what you are going to do during your stay, plus being aware of the weather, will make a big difference. Peru has such a variable climate and vast landscape, from mountains to beaches to sand dunes. So, plan ahead of time. Will you be hiking, surfing, or taking a ride in dune buggies? Because, honestly, you can do them all in Peru! And, well, we basically did!

Peru does have a rainy season, so if you want to hike Machu Picchu or Rainbow Mountain, going in the rainy season would not be recommended. They literally have grates on top of Machu Picchu so you don't slip and slide down. Although the ground stays intact during that season, I personally would not want to be there during that time frame. After doing my research, I found September to be the perfect climate for us—it also happened to be my birthday month. Yippee! And it was perfect. The weather was warmer down in Miraflores where we stayed the majority of the time, and then it was cooler when we flew up to Cusco for the hike. Obviously, up in the mountains, it was chillier. But it was still a perfect day for us. I honestly couldn't have asked for a better day to be on top of a mountain. Here is a basic rundown of the seasons in Peru:

Dry Season (May to October)

The best time to hike in Peru, especially if Machu Picchu is on your list, is during the dry season from May to October. These months offer the clearest skies and the least likelihood of rain, providing safer and more enjoyable hiking conditions. The temperatures during these months are generally cooler, which can be a relief during strenuous hikes.

- **Peak Months**: June to August marks the peak tourist season. Expect the trails to be busier and for Machu Picchu to be teeming with visitors. If you aim to avoid the crowds while still enjoying the benefits of the dry season, consider planning your hike in May or late September to early October. We still had crowds, and we went at the end of September. So, honestly, I think tourists will always be there.

Shoulder Months (April and November)

- **April** and **November** serve as transition periods and can offer a balance between favorable weather and thinner crowds. While there's a higher chance of rain compared to the dry season, the trails are less crowded, offering a more serene experience.

- **Weather Variability**: Keep in mind that weather in the Andes can be unpredictable. Even during the dry season, it's wise to be prepared for occasional showers and cold nights.

I honestly thought September was perfect. Temperatures were in the mid-sixties during the day. When the sun was out, it was absolutely beautiful. At nighttime, it was a tad chillier and would drop down into the forties and fifties. However, down in the Lima/Miraflores area, it was fairly humid. The heat of the tropical sun is moderated by the cold Humboldt Current that flows northward along the coast of Peru. This keeps temperatures in the city mild with almost no rain and high humidity year-round. While this sounds great on the surface, these weather factors also lead to mold growth. I'll dive deeper into this when we explore the "Where to Stay" chapter.

I'm used to high humidity since I'm from Florida, but this area had a wet-cold environment, closer to California in the wintertime. Actually, a lot of it reminded me of California. The fact that you can go hiking one day on a mountain top, go surfing another, and then go to the desert; everything is just a few hours away. Definitely Cali vibes! This is definitely cold, wet, and humid, so bring warm clothes. Yes, I'm a Florida girl, and I wore my winter clothes, hahaha.

Chapter 4 Where to Stay

I did a lot of research prior to our month-long adventure in Peru. Neither one of us had been there prior to deciding to stay for an entire month. A hotel was going to be a tad expensive, so I went to Airbnb to look for an apartment to rent. For something this extensive, I wanted a kitchen and a living room where we could cook, hang out, and have our own bedrooms. I love going to new countries and living like locals; shopping where they shop, hanging out where they do, and just immersing yourself in the city and culture. Jeff and I did this exact same thing country-hopping in Asia for four months—that was actually where we met and became friends back in 2019. Each month included visiting a different country and living in a different apartment. From floating cities in Vietnam to elephant sanctuaries in Thailand, it was an amazing experience; I was looking to recreate that. Honestly, I've been itching to country-hop ever since 2019, but COVID put a big damper on that. Since then, I've slowly been getting back into it. It's 2024—here I am, writing my second travel book; we thought that nasty global pandemic was only going to last a summer.

Sigh.

I looked at multiple areas in Peru and then eventually booked an apartment in Miraflores. I wanted something nice, safe, within walking distance to lots of places, and with a gorgeous view. Here are the top places I would recommend to stay.

Miraflores

Nestled along the stunning Pacific coastline, Miraflores stands as one of Lima's most vibrant and picturesque districts. Miraflores is widely regarded as one of the safest areas in Lima for tourists. Its well-lit streets, constant police presence, and CCTV coverage ensure that visitors can explore with peace of mind. When it comes to finding a place to stay, Miraflores offers a range of options, from luxury hotels with ocean views to cozy hostels and apartments, catering to all preferences and budgets. There were literally always police officers on every corner. I always felt safe walking around night or day. Grocery stores, restaurants, nightlife, and the ocean were all at your fingertips. It was about a forty-five-minute cab ride from the airport to get there early in the morning.

Key Attractions in Miraflores

1. Parque Kennedy

Center to Miraflores' buzzing life, Parque Kennedy is not just a park but a cultural hub. Surrounded by cafes, street vendors, and occasionally, art fairs, t's a perfect spot to immerse yourself in the local vibe. Don't miss the multitude of friendly, local cats who've made this park their home! I loved coming here and playing with the cats because I miss my baby Callie, who passed away in 2021. These cats are amazingly clean and don't look feral or nasty.

2. Larcomar Shopping Center

Perched on a cliff overlooking the Pacific Ocean, Larcomar is not your typical shopping center. It offers a unique blend of shopping, entertainment, and dining experiences, all with a breathtaking view of the sea. It's a fantastic place to shop for local brands and international labels, catch a movie, or enjoy sunset dinners.

3. Malecón de Miraflores

The Malecón, a boardwalk stretching over six miles along the cliff's edge, provides panoramic views of the Pacific Ocean. It's ideal for a leisurely walk, bike ride, or a moment to watch paragliders soar above. The park-lined boardwalk is also home to sculptures, outdoor gyms, and beautifully landscaped gardens.

4. Huaca Pucllana

This pre-Incan adobe pyramid, nestled in the heart of Miraflores, offers a fascinating glimpse into ancient Lima cultures. Guided tours of the site shed light on its historical significance and the civilizations that built it. The on-site restaurant serves contemporary Peruvian cuisine with a view of the illuminated ruins at night.

Barranco

Known as the SoHo of Lima, *Barranco* is one of the city's hippest neighborhoods. If you want more nightlife, then discover the enchanting district of Barranco in Lima, Peru, where art, culture, and history come alive against the backdrop of breathtaking Pacific Ocean views. Known as the cultural heart of Lima, Barranco is a must-visit for anyone who wants to experience the city's bohemian side. With its array of attractions, from vibrant street art to historic buildings, Barranco offers a unique blend of experiences that captivate all who wander its colorful streets.

Barranco provides a wide range of accommodation options, from luxurious hotels to cozy hostels that cater to every type of traveler. Staying in Barranco is highly recommended to fully immerse yourself in the district's vibrant life and to have easy access to its many attractions.

Some top accommodations in Barranco include:

- **Hotel B**: A boutique, luxury hotel offering exquisite rooms and unmatched service, located close to all major attractions in Barranco.

- **Casa República Barranco**: A beautifully restored 1920s mansion-turned-hotel, combining the charm of a bygone era with modern comforts and elegance. This is a beautiful hotel with a high-end style.

- **The Point Hostel Lima**: For travelers on a budget, The Point offers a friendly and social atmosphere, comfortable accommodations, and a short walk from the beach and Barranco's nightlife. This option is definitely for the younger crowd looking for a party atmosphere or solo travelers wanting to meet new people.

Key Attractions in Barranco

1. Puente de Los Suspiros (Bridge of Sighs)

No visit to Barranco is complete without a stroll across the iconic Puente de Los Suspiros. Legend has it that if you hold your breath while crossing the bridge for the first time and make a wish, it will come true. The area around the bridge is also perfect for exploring, with numerous cafés, bars, and street performers adding to the lively atmosphere.

2. Plaza de Barranco

The heart of Barranco, Plaza de Barranco, is surrounded by some of the district's most picturesque architecture. It is a hub of activity both day and night. The plaza is home to the beautiful Iglesia La Ermita, whose mysterious past and stunning murals are bound to enchant any visitor.

3. MATE - Museo Mario Testino

Art enthusiasts will not want to miss MATE, the museum dedicated to Peru's most famous photographer, Mario Testino. This vibrant space showcases not only Testino's globally recognized work, including images of international celebrities and models, but also features exhibitions by other Peruvian artists, providing a glimpse into the country's rich artistic heritage.

4. Bajada de Baños

This charming walkway offers picturesque views and leads visitors from the town down to the Pacific Ocean. Along the way, you'll pass by quaint houses, art galleries, and lush vegetation. The path perfectly captures the coastal charm of Barranco.

5. Dédalo Arte y Artesanía

For those interested in taking a piece of Barranco home with them, Dédalo Arte y Artesanía offers a wide range of handmade Peruvian crafts, jewelry, and art. This market is a treasure trove of unique finds and is an ideal place for souvenirs and gifts.

San Isidro

If you are looking for the Miami vibe, go to San Isidro. Nestled in the vibrant heart of Peru, it has long been recognized as one of Lima's most prestigious districts. It's a haven where modernity seamlessly blends with tradition, offering visitors a unique experience that captivates the elite traveler. Explore the must-visit attractions and indulge in the local cuisine of this distinguished locale to make your stay truly unforgettable. The streets are lined with exotic cars, skyscrapers, and more, so your hotels will reflect that price here. My travel buddy Jeff had one free night on his Hilton Rewards, so he cashed it in here; we lived it up and rubbed shoulders with the rich and famous for a night in the desirable San Isidro district. Well, he stayed in his fancy hotel, but I Ubered it back to my shabby Miraflores apartment. Funny thing was, my "Uber" was a rusted-out, Toyota-something that was falling apart. The hotel doorman was so polite and even confirmed the Uber for me from my phone, checked the license plate, and confirmed the driver was legit before I got in. I received very nice service from this five-star hotel. Nonetheless, I was embarrassed getting into the rust bucket as the doorman with his white gloves opened the door for me. However, I do have to say that it was the most fun Uber ride I have ever had in my life, so don't judge a book by its cover. (Unless you're buying this book, then do!). This Uber driver only spoke Spanish, and I only spoke broken Spanglish. During the ride, he asked me what kind of music I wanted to listen to and, well, I didn't care. So, he put on one of his favorites and serenaded me the entire drive home. It was the cutest thing ever.

Key Attractions in San Isidro

1. Huaca Huallamarca

An ancient pyramid right in the heart of San Isidro, Huaca Huallamarca stands as a testament to Peru's rich, pre-Columbian history. Once a ceremonial and burial site, it now beckons history buffs and the culturally curious to explore its museum and the preserved remains of its past.

2. El Olivar Park

This serene oasis, with its sprawling olive grove, offers a tranquil escape from the city's hustle and bustle. Dating back to the 16th century, the park not only provides lush landscapes and walking paths but also serves as a reminder of the area's agricultural heritage.

    3. **Golf Club**

Golf enthusiasts will find solace and challenge at the Lima Golf Club in San Isidro. Its meticulously maintained greens and fairways make for an enjoyable day on the course amidst the backdrop of the city's skyline.

Cusco

Nestled in the heart of the Peruvian Andes, Cusco is a city that vibrates with the echoes of its past. Once the capital of the Inca Empire, one of the most powerful and sophisticated pre-Columbian civilizations in the Americas, Cusco's history is a fascinating blend of Indigenous cultures, colonial conquests, and modern transformations. This vibrant city, declared a UNESCO World Heritage Site in 1983, serves as a living museum that continues to captivate visitors with its enduring legacy.

In modern times, Cusco has emerged as a key destination for cultural and adventure tourism, serving as the gateway to the sacred valley and the iconic Machu Picchu. The city itself offers a vivid tableau of its layered history, where cobblestone streets lead to Incan ruins, colonial churches, and vibrant markets selling traditional textiles and crafts.

Tourism has brought both prosperity and challenges to Cusco. Efforts are underway to protect the city's precious heritage while accommodating the needs of the millions who come to experience its magic each year. Through initiatives like sustainable tourism and cultural preservation programs, Cusco strives to maintain its identity amidst the forces of globalization.

Going to the capitol, Cusco, is like going back in time. If you are going to hike Machu Picchu, you will definitely spend some time in Cusco. You need to just acclimate to the altitude before you hike and experience the difference in culture from Lima. The interesting thing is, I didn't get as much altitude sickness as Jeff did when we went. I'm prone to motion sickness, so I was afraid I would be more sensitive to it; however, Jeff was more prone to the illness than I was during the trip. They have these tea leaves you can drink to manage the symptoms, and Jeff kept drinking it. I didn't even need it. I just felt like I had a little buzz after having a glass of wine, so it didn't bother me much. Something I discovered later was that, apparently, younger people are more prone to altitude sickness versus older people. Maybe one good thing about getting older! I was forty-five at the time, and Jeff was thirty. So, maybe that's why?

We stayed in a hotel that was prearranged by the travel company we used to book the entire trip for Machu Picchu— I will explain that entire process later. I do not recommend planning that on your own, though; too many logistics. Anyway, it was a super cute boutique hotel within walking distance of the city center. If you are going to stay in Cusco at all, I recommend booking in advance. It's not a big area, so accommodations can fill up fast. When we arrived and we were walking around the city center, there was a travel agency just jam-packed with backpackers waiting in line. I'm way too Type A personality to wait until the last minute to plan anything. But apparently, many other people are too. I hope all those people smashed in that office found what they were waiting for.

Some top accommodations in Cusco include:

1. **San Francisco Plaza Cusco.** This is where we stayed. It was nice that breakfast was included. It was an interesting breakfast; I recall having fruit, rice, pancakes, coffee, and other things at the buffet I didn't recognize. Jeff had some fruit I didn't want to try. They also gave us a paper bag breakfast the morning of our hike because we had to leave at like 5 AM.
2. **Hilton Garden Inn Cusco.** Yes, there is a Hilton in Cusco, and it actually isn't priced too bad either.
3. **JW Marriott.** Great if you want to go fancy; it's also directly in the City Center. But it's definitely pricey.
4. There are lots of hostels and much cheaper local stays, but I would do my research first.

Our Hotel San Francisco Plaza Cusco

Chapter 5 Scams in Peru

Peru, a country known for its breathtaking landscapes, rich history, and vibrant culture, attracts visitors from all over the world. However, like any popular travel destination, it comes with its own set of challenges, particularly when it comes to navigating potential scams. A common scam that travelers in Peru might encounter involves the Indigenous people and getting you to take photos with the adorable alpacas. Here are some tips on how to protect yourself from this and other scams, ensuring your visit is both enjoyable and safe.

We actually were a victim of this scam while we were in Cusco. Funny enough, we had been living in Peru for almost a month and had not been a victim of any scams, really, other than the mold issue in the Airbnb. That was more of a building issue, though. If a building doesn't have central heat and air, it's not the owners' fault, but they should still do more to rectify the issues in their own unit. However, we had not been flat out targeted until we arrived in Cusco at the very end of our trip. Maybe because it's a much more tourist populated area? I'm not sure. However, just beware, and keep your eyes open.

The first scam we fell into was when a group of Indigenous ladies were walking around the city center with the most adorable alpacas and a baby alpaca. In this type of scam, they'll come up to you and ask if you want to take a photo. How can you say no to this face? I mean, come on! Of course I wanted to take a picture! And they are, OMG, sooooo soft. You definitely should buy some blankets or sweaters made from alpaca fur; it is the most divine thing ever. I gave Jeff my iPhone, and he started taking some pictures. They said some amount in Peruvian soles, but I was so

distracted by the animals that I wasn't paying much attention. Then, more ladies come over and hand you the baby alpaca to hold. Once they snag a live one—a happy tourist—then they all come over. Then they ask if you want a photo together, and they take your iPhone. They take a bunch of photos. Once you try to leave, they will not give you your iPhone back. Now, the price has gone way up. Why? Oh, because they didn't tell you it was more for the baby alpaca and more for each photo. So, I'm like what, WTF is going on, are you kidding me right now? Just give me my damn iPhone back. I start arguing with the ladies, all five-foot tall. They start getting in my face and surrounding me, and I'm like, what the hell is going on here, this is crazy. At this point, I just want my iPhone back, so I dump all my Sol coins into the ladies' hands in order to get my iPhone back, and I say, "This is all I have. I have no more money!" Which was almost the truth; I had paper money, but I just wasn't going to open my purse to get even more money. I have traveled enough, so I separate my cash out just for crazy events like this. I showed no more money. The one lady gave me my iPhone back. I'm like, oh thank God, and we started walking away. Then the other ladies started to surround me and said, "Oh, that's just for her, now we need our money."

I yelled back as we pushed through them, and I'm like, "oh hell no! That's for all y'all!" Then a police officer came up and started speaking to them in Spanish, and they quicky dispersed. This is obviously a scam they do frequently to tourists. So, if you want a picture with an alpaca, do not ever, by any means, hand over your cell phone! In retrospect, I probably only paid 5 USD, which was fine. That part didn't bother me, it was the bait and switch that was not cool. I don't mind paying them for a photo, just don't threaten me. I took pictures with a sloth in Haiti and that was an upfront, pay for what you get, transaction. Just be honest is all I ask.

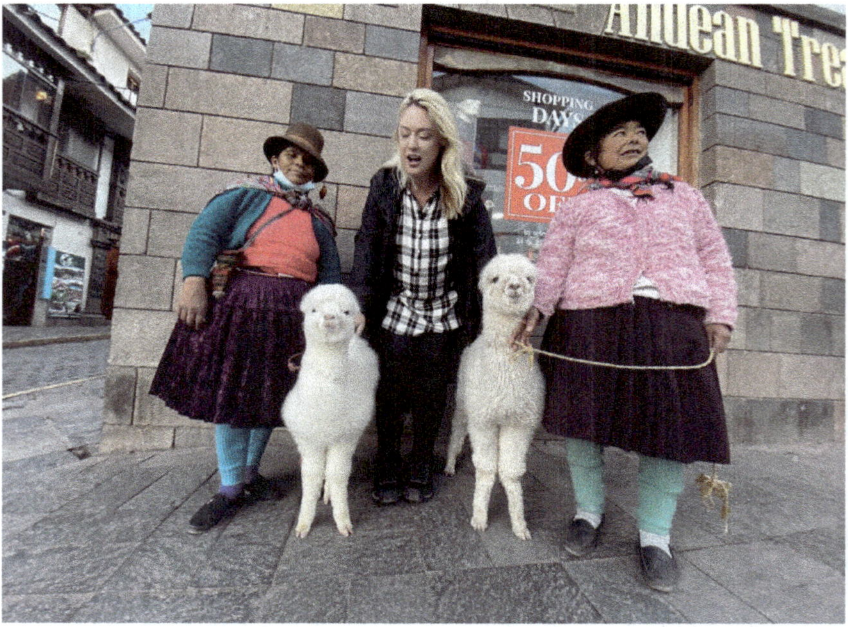
SHOPPING DAYS

Ca. Plateros
Andean Treas
SHOPPING DAYS
50%

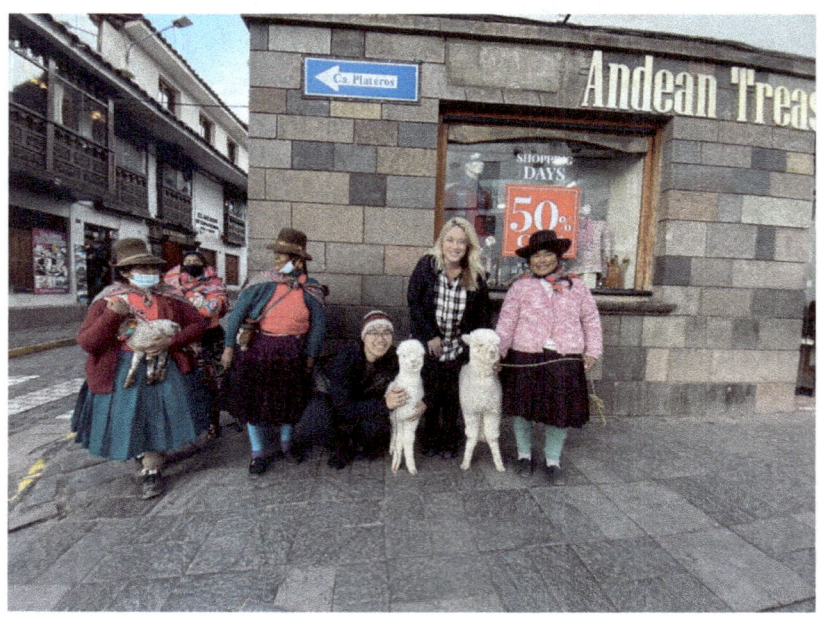

Local Restaurants

For the most part, the local restaurants were very friendly and welcoming to us. However, some locals don't like the tourists being in their town. I always like to visit the local places and try the mom-and-pop stores when I am traveling. We were craving chicken at the moment and looked up a local place. A Peruvian staple is chicken and French fries. So, we looked up a place to get some chicken. We found PIO'S CHICKEN. Unfortunately, we didn't read the reviews first. We walked in, and they seated us and gave us menus. We sat down and looked at the menu. The place was busy, so we figured it was good. Well, we sat there forever. We watched our waiter literally wait on every table around us, but never stop at our table. We obviously were tourists in a local place. Jeff and I stick out like sore thumbs. I'm a blonde, White woman, he is an Asian man, and we do not look Peruvian by any means. However, we are still paying customers. Even a local guy eating across from us noticed the lack of customer service and said something to the waiter. Then, he finally brought us some water. We were hoping he was going to pay attention to us, but no. Instead, we watched people come in, sit down, order, eat their food, and leave, and we still had not had the opportunity to even place our order. I'm like, this is bullshit. After the ENTIRE restaurant emptied out and new people came in, we still had not placed our order; it was obvious they don't like tourists and, apparently, they didn't want our money, either. So, we got up and walked out.

Now, this place was one where you paid on the way out. So, the cashier placed at the entrance had no idea that we never got food. As we walked past her, she started yelling at us that we needed to pay. Jeff just walked right out. Then the waiter came chasing after us. LOL, why? I have no idea. For the waters? Those were not bottled, mind you. I was so pissed off; I, at least, knew some Spanglish, so I just yelled back, "No comida! No comida!" I couldn't get into the details of how horrible the customer service was because my four years of Spanish classes were not *that good*. I am not fluent. And then I walked out, too. We were still craving chicken, so we found a KFC. Not exactly the local flair we were looking for, but at least they treated us like regular customers.

Google Reviews below for PIO'S CHICKEN:

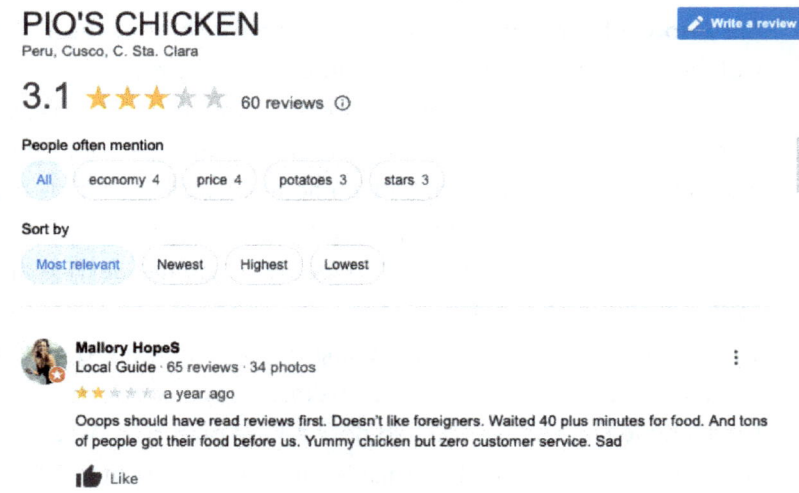

PIO'S CHICKEN
Peru, Cusco, C. Sta. Clara

3.1 ★★★☆☆ 60 reviews ⓘ

Kevin Guardia
7 reviews · 2 photos
★☆☆☆☆ 2 years ago

In reality, the service is terrible, the food is horrible, the potatoes are hard as a stone, the soup looks like unsalted water, the chicken has feathers, honestly you should inspect the place, both national and foreign tourists come in to lock for meals that represent, but The attention is even terrible, they give a bad impression to Cusco

Translated by Google · See original (Spanish)

👍 2

PIO'S CHICKEN
Peru, Cusco, C. Sta. Clara

3.1 ★★★☆☆ 60 reviews ⓘ

You had ordered the raw chicken with bye and because they ran out they served us right after I complained and told us it was over and they charged us the same as if they had given us bye. No more return.

Translated by Google · See original (Spanish)

👍 Like

Marianna Gonzales
2 reviews
★☆☆☆☆ 2 years ago

I give it one star because I can't give it less, the food was terrible, tasteless, the potatoes looked like they were saved, the chicken had no flavor and was raw, the service is terrible, if they don't want to work there is no reason to mistreat the diners Not to mention that both the premises and the workers were in very poor conditions and without complying with any health protocol. To top it all off, we were waiting almost an hour for a soft drink that never arrived. When we went to the kitchen to demand it, they rudely handed us a liquid similar to dirty water.

Translated by Google · See original (Spanish)

It's funny to see a bucket of KCF chicken by Machu Picchu.

Chapter 6 Cell Phones & Traveling

You definitely are going to need your smartphone when you are traveling abroad. For tickets, maps, getting cars, texting, and basically everything else we do in life. Without a phone, you are walking blind in another country. You really do need Google Maps to figure out where the hell you are. You will also need the Google Translate app and so many other things. It's better to get a local SIM card versus relying on your provider when abroad. It's going to be much cheaper, and you will have way better service. Here's why: I have T-Mobile. When I lived in Asia for four months, I called them before I left. They said it was going to work in Asia, no problem. WRONG. It didn't work at all. I was so pissed. I was on the phone with them for hours yelling at them once I arrived in Vietnam, blind, without a working cell phone. The only time it did work was when I was in my apartment connected to Wi-Fi. Thankfully, I had free calls over Wi-Fi. Anyways, I had to spend four hours on the phone with customer service to get them to jail break my phone for me to utilize a local SIM card for the rest of my trip. This situation caused me a lot of headaches in the first couple of days. Thankfully, I brought two phones with me on that trip: my work cell and my personal cell. I got a local SIM card on my personal to use while I was out and about for maps, walking, etcetera, and left the work one at the apartment. Then I used that one on Wi-Fi to call clients and text friends and family back home on a Florida phone number. It actually worked out great for biz purposes because when I was making client calls from Vietnam, it still came through as my 727-area code, so they had no idea I was in Hanoi and not in my Florida office.

Now, every time I travel to another country, I always get a local SIM card *before I leave* to avoid this headache. The other thing is, even if your local provider like AT&T or Verizon *might* work overseas, you might either get bad service, or they might even bill you for extra roaming fees. Did you hear about the couple that went to Switzerland and came back with a $143,000 cell phone bill?! He was also on T-Mobile. Well, they did the same thing as me. Anyways, he called in first and told them he was traveling. He asked if his phone would work there, and they said yes. Well, his phone DID work, yet they charged him up the wazoo in fees!

"Rene Remund told WFTS he was charged $143,269 for using 9.5 gigabytes of roaming data during a three-week trip to Switzerland" https://www.wilx.com/2024/04/19/man-shocked-by-143000-phone-bill-overseas-trip/

Do yourself a favor and just get a local SIM card instead. Spending $40 instead of $143,000 will be easier on your wallet! If you have a newer smartphone, now you can actually get eSIM cards, and it makes the process even easier than before. For example, if you have an iPhone 11 or newer, they support the eSIM. That means you can just download an app, get the country that you are going to, and get it before you even arrive. Then, you are ready to go once your feet hit the soil. This is super helpful because when I landed in Peru, I had a ride already arranged for me by my Airbnb. However, I was going to get a physical SIM card when I landed in the airport. That's what I did when country-hopping through Asia and Greece. If you have an older smartphone, you will have to do that as well, which I will talk about in the next section. But in Peru, there was only one kiosk selling SIM cards, and they wanted over $100, which is a total rip-off. Normally, for a month of service, it's like $40. No way was I going to pay that amount of money. So, I skipped it. But then I was blindly walking out of the airport, my iPhone didn't work, I couldn't find my ride, and there was no Wi-Fi. UGH!

Most international airports have multiple SIM card kiosks that you can choose from that will help you buy and install a local SIM card into your phone before you enter the country. Peru was the first time I experienced this inconvenience. So, definitely download the app if you have a newer smartphone and get the eSIM before you arrive in Peru. I used the Airalo app. Then, choose your country and how much data you want. For Peru, it was $20 for five gigabytes. Then, you can top it off as needed.

https://www.airalo.com/global-esim   *These plans are prices based on 2024*

Use code TARA9517 when you sign up or apply it at checkout & get $3 off your eSIM card!

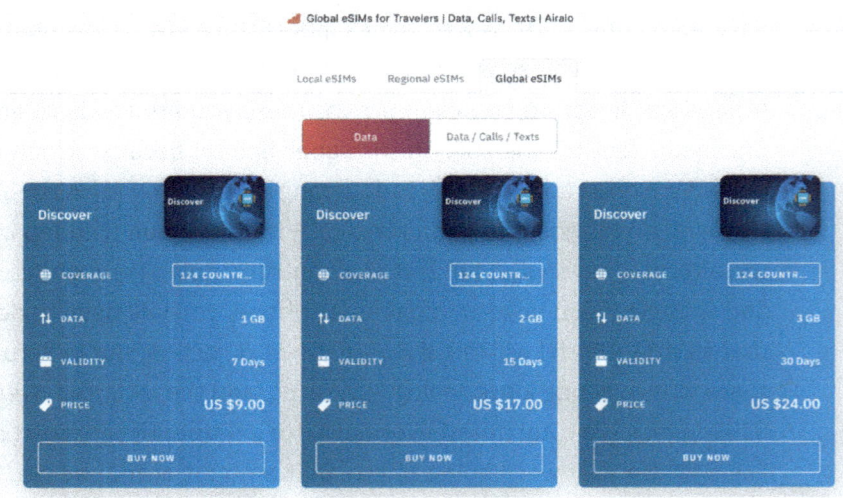

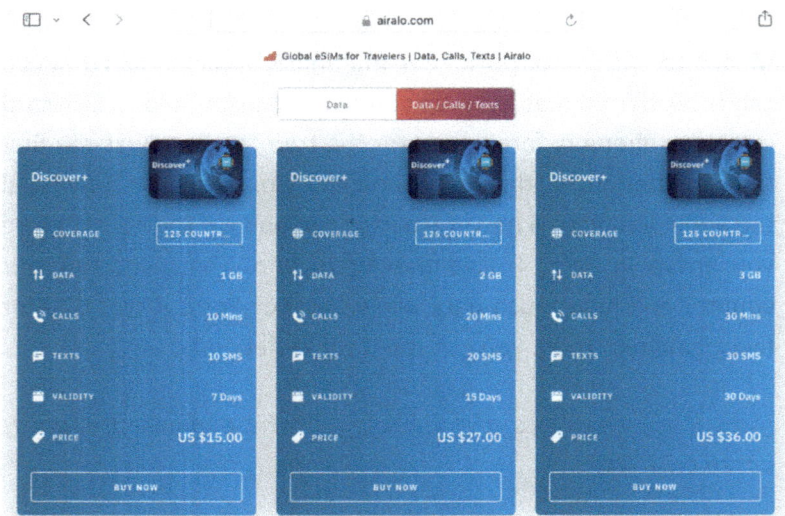

How Airalo Works

Download the app

Choose your destination and package

Install your eSIM

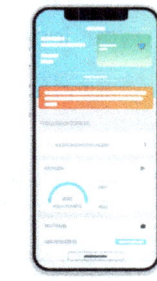
Activate your eSIM

It looks like you can just get a global plan as well if you are globe-trotting, and it's cheaper if you just get a data plan versus calling and texting. What I do is install https://www.whatsapp.com on my phone when traveling abroad. I tell family to contact me there or on Facebook messenger. Another good rule of thumb—and why you should always have WhatsApp on your phone when traveling—is that most other countries use this as their main way of communicating. When we were island hopping through Greece, every single host on Airbnb sent messengers to us via WhatsApp. I had cab drivers call me through that app. It's free and, yes, you can call and text through it because it basically just uses the Wi-Fi connection instead of cellular data. So, do yourself a favor and install that at home on your phone before you land. I was happy I did when we arrived in Greece with our pre-arranged taxi ride to our Airbnb because he called me on it to find out where we were and why we were taking so long. It was because I was waiting in line to get my SIM card installed, LOL.

Installing a Physical SIM Card

If you have an older smartphone, you will need to use a physical SIM card. Here are some photos and short instructions if you have to do it yourself. In most kiosks, they will do it for you, so you do not have to. But when you get home, you will have to reinstall your local SIM card back in.

Locate the SIM card slot on the right hand side of your iPhone. It might be a different location for other phones. Use something small to put into the hole to pop the tray open.

Replace your SIM with the new SIM. Make sure to put it in the correct way. There is a corner cut to show you how. Then just reinsert it back into your iPhone. Keep your SIM card in a SAFE place & don't loose it while traveling so you can replace it when back home.

Keeping Your Phone Safe While Traveling Abroad

Losing your smartphone, even when you are at home, is a tragedy. Yet, if you do when you are abroad, it can be like losing an arm. You need this for everything! It's your map for walking around, getting rides, for your translation apps, and so much more. And it seems that phone thefts are on the rise, so be careful. When you are out of the country, you cannot just go out and get another iPhone. If you are in Japan, they will sell iPhones in Japanese, Greek, etc. That is, if you are even lucky enough to find an Apple store because they are not everywhere around the world.

For example, when we were traveling throughout Asia, a couple of different people broke their iPhones and couldn't replace them because there were no Apple stores in Vietnam or Thailand. Jeff, once he landed in Vietnam, was looking at his phone for the map for walking directions, and then a Vietnamese guy on a motorbike drove by and literally grabbed it and almost pulled it out of his hands. That was on the second day of a four-month trip! Can you imagine having your phone stolen that early on? I have gotten in the habit of traveling with two phones for this very reason, with my personal phone and my business phone. I leave the business one in the hotel and take my personal one out with me. This way, I always have a backup just in case something happens. Hopefully, nothing does, but we rely on our technology so much in this day and age that it's not a bad idea to bring an old phone with you if you have one lying around on your next trip.

These devices are not just means of communication; they are vaults of sensitive information from bank details to personal photos. Here are comprehensive tips to keep your phone safe from theft and unauthorized access when you are exploring new territories:

1. Stay Aware of Your Surroundings

The most straightforward yet crucial piece of advice is to always be aware of your surroundings. Thieves often target travelers who seem distracted or unaware. When using your phone in public spaces, keep a tight grip on it, and avoid pulling it out in crowded areas where people can easily snatch it from your hand. Even when I am traveling in the States, I don't like to look like I have no idea where I am going because it makes me a target. So, I will take a quick look at, say, walking directions, and then put my phone away so my eye and head are up and looking at the people and my surroundings, not buried in my phone.

2. Use a Sturdy Phone Case with a Strap

Invest in a robust phone case that can protect your device from drops and shocks. Many cases also come with straps or lanyards. Wearing your phone around your neck or wrist can deter snatch-and-grab attempts, making it harder for thieves to run off with your device.

3. Keep Your Phone Secured When Not in Use

When you're not using your phone, keep it securely stored in a zipped pocket or a bag that stays close to your body. Consider using bags with hidden or internal pockets that aren't easily accessible to pickpockets such as your back pocket.

4. Use Biometric and Password Protections

Secure your phone with biometric locks (fingerprint or facial recognition) and a strong password or PIN. In case your phone does get stolen, these measures can help prevent unauthorized access to your personal information.

5. Enable 'Find My Device' Features

Before heading abroad, make sure to enable any 'find my device' features that your smartphone may offer. These services allow you to track your phone's location, remotely lock it, or even wipe its data if it gets stolen.

6. Be Cautious with Public Wi-Fi

While abroad, you may be tempted to use public Wi-Fi to save on data costs. However, public networks can be insecure. If you must use them, avoid accessing sensitive information like bank accounts. Consider using a Virtual Private Network (VPN) to encrypt your data and protect your online activities.

7. Make a Digital Copy of Important Documents

Use your phone to keep digital copies of important documents like your passport, visa, and itinerary. However, ensure these documents are stored securely, either in a password-protected folder on your device or in a secure cloud storage service.

8. Avoid Using Your Phone in High-Risk Areas

Be mindful of where and when you use your phone. In areas known for high theft rates or at night, it may be safer to keep your phone out of sight to avoid drawing attention. Also, don't just leave your phone out on the table at a café or bar. At home we are used to doing this, yet in a different country and tourist area, I would be cautious of leaving it in plain sight. Be cautious even when riding in Ubers. I have heard stories of people in Peru riding a car with the window down and a person walking by reaches in, grabs their phone, and then runs off.

9. Keep Emergency Numbers Handy

Write down local emergency numbers on a piece of paper as soon as you arrive at your destination, including the local police and embassy or consulate. This can be incredibly useful in case of emergency or if your phone is stolen. I aways keep these handy as well as my hotel name, address, and copies of my passports in an envelope. Having paper copies of everything is super helpful just in case of worst-case scenarios.

10. Regularly Back up Your Data

Regularly back up your photos, contacts, and other important data. Whether you're using cloud storage or a physical computer, having backups ensures that you won't lose everything if your phone is lost or stolen.

By following these tips, you can significantly reduce the risks associated with carrying a smartphone while traveling abroad. Remember, preparation and vigilance are key to ensuring your travels are safe and enjoyable, without unwanted interruptions.

Taxis in Peru

When getting around Peru, there are multiple ways to get a ride. You can download and utilize the Uber app; it is not banned like in other countries. So, go ahead and utilize it in Peru. They also have private taxis and public taxis. Now, the public taxis are dodgy and not regulated, so I would steer clear of them. They do not use meters and usually rip off tourists. You can tell which taxis are privately regulated because they wear a uniform that is all blue. They tend to wear a blue sweater, slacks, and have a badge with their ID around their necks. The one thing about Peru is they are all about formalities and uniforms. If someone is wearing a uniform, they are usually official and legit.

If you do not have a prearranged ride when arriving at the airport in Lima, then one-hundred-some guys will bum rush you for a taxi ride as you exit the airport. No joke. It's totally insane; I have never seen anything like it before. I had a prearranged ride, but I couldn't find him in the sea of other men. I felt like I was in the middle of a rock concert. My prearranged ride was very reasonably priced because I booked it in advance. When I couldn't find him, and then my phone didn't work to text or call the guy since I didn't get a local SIM card yet, I didn't know what to do. Eventually, I ended up getting one of the private taxis instead. It was about a forty-five-minute drive to Miraflores from the airport, and it cost me triple.

.

Chapter 7 Protests in Peru & Political Unrest

On a cool, breezy morning, I was working from the balcony of our Airbnb when a commotion got my attention. A huge group of Peruvians marched down the streets of Miraflores along the coastline. They had signs and chanted in Spanish. Unfortunately, my Spanglish and classes from high school didn't help me understand what they were saying. I did take a video though, which helped me google what was on the signs to figure out what they were protesting.

Protests seem to be a common thing in Peru. While we were visiting, we witnessed many protests, but thankfully, they were peaceful in nature. The protests that we saw back in 2022 were about the president elected at the time. It was eerily similar to the political climate of America. The Peruvian people believed that the current president elect had stolen the election and won illegally. Pedro Castillo's presidency, which began in July 2021, faced significant opposition and controversy. His administration saw recurring clashes with Congress, accusations of corruption, and multiple attempts at impeachment. This tumultuous governance sparked feelings of mistrust and disillusionment, further fueling protests as citizens demanded stability and accountability. They wanted change.

When we visited the capital area of Lima, we witnessed more protests in that area. There was a lot more police presence there, but it still wasn't violent. I never felt unsafe, as they were protesting for their country, and we were just visitors. But after we left Peru, this took a turn for the worse. Pedro Castillo was ousted as president of Peru on December 7, 2022, following an impeachment vote by Congress after his attempted dissolution of the legislative body. He was attempting to illegally dismantle his own Congress. However, without the backing of the military and his own political party, they went after him. He fled to seek asylum at the Mexican Embassy when he got stuck in traffic and was arrested.

A series of political protests against the government of President Dina Boluarte and the Congress of Peru occurred. The demonstrations lack centralized leadership and originated primarily among grassroots movements and social organizations on the left to far-left, as well as Indigenous communities, who feel politically disenfranchised. Castillo was removed from office and arrested after announcing the illegal dissolution of Congress, the intervention of the state apparatus, and the forced establishment of an "emergency government", which was characterized as a self-coup attempt by all government institutions, all professional institutions, and mainstream media in Peru (and by the international community in general) while Castillo's supporters said that Congress attempted to overthrow Castillo. Castillo's successor, Dina Boluarte, along with Congress, were widely disapproved, with the two receiving the lowest approval ratings among public offices in the Americas. Among the main demands of the demonstrators are the dissolution of Congress, the resignation of Boluarte, new general elections, the release of Castillo, and the formation of a constituent assembly to draft a new constitution. It has also been reported that some of the protesters have declared an insurgency in Punos's region. Analysts, businesses, and voters said that immediate elections are necessary to prevent future unrest, although many established political parties have little public support.

The Boluarte government would respond to protests by calling the protests a "threat to democracy" and announcing a national state of emergency on 14 December, suspending some constitutional rights of citizens, including the right to preventing troops from staying within private homes and buildings, the right to freedom of movement, the right to freedom of assembly, and the right to "personal freedom and security" for 30 days. The Armed Forces and Police have been documented using severe force against the protesters, resulting in at least 60 deaths, over 600 injuries, over 380 some arrests, and two massacres in Ayacucho and Juliaca. The extra judicial executions, use of torture, and violence against detainees, have also been reported. The government would deny that authorities acted violently and would instead praise officers and troops for their actions. (source: Wikipedia)

What I read in the expat forums on Facebook after I was home was that many roads were closed down due to these violent protests. They attacked innocent people who were driving ambulances with injured people in them. One carried a girl who needed medical attention, and the protesters wouldn't let the ambulance through. I can't remember what happened to the little girl, but they said they were throwing rocks at it. Why? So senseless. Travelers from other countries had to be evacuated in an emergency-type situation with their own country sending planes in to get them from Cusco. I remember seeing it on the news here in Florida and being so sad since I had just been there. It's crazy how a climate can change that fast. Many touring companies had to cancel their trips. I was actually in the process of planning a writing retreat in Machu Picchu, and I had to cancel my plans as well because it became too scary.

Peru has had a history of an unstable political climate and an interesting list of past presidents. Peru has never had a "Japanese President" per se. However, Alberto Fujimori, who served as the President of Peru from 1990 to 2000, was of Japanese descent. Born in Lima, Peru, to Japanese immigrant parents, Fujimori was the first person of East Asian heritage to become a head of state in Latin America.

Fujimori's presidency was marked by both significant economic reforms and serious controversies, including allegations of corruption, human rights abuses, and authoritarian measures. After resigning in 2000, he fled to Japan, where he claimed citizenship due to his heritage. In April 2009, Fujimori was convicted of human rights violations and sentenced to 25 years in prison for his role in killings and kidnappings by the Grupo Colina death squad during his government's battle against far-left guerrillas in the 1990s. Despite his mixed legacy, Fujimori remains an important historical figure in both Peru and the global Japanese diaspora.

Throughout the 20th century, Japanese immigration to Peru played a significant role in shaping the country's culture and society. In the late 1800s, Peru experienced a labor shortage due to the end of slavery and growing demand for agricultural workers. To fill this gap, Peruvian authorities encouraged Japanese farmers to immigrate to Peru, offering them land and other incentives.

Over the next several decades, thousands of Japanese immigrants arrived in Peru, settling primarily in coastal areas where they established successful farms and businesses. Despite facing discrimination and prejudice from other ethnic groups, many Japanese Peruvians thrived and eventually integrated into mainstream Peruvian society. (Wikipedia)

Today, Peru is home to one of the largest Japanese diaspora, so you can find the most authentic Japanese food in Peru, which left me surprised. And very happy, too, to say the least, since I lived in Japan for a few months back in 2019. I absolutely love Japanese food! So, this was a really cool thing to discover.

I don't want to tell you these stories to scare you from traveling to Peru or other countries; it's more so to be aware before you do and when you are there. You never know how things can change at any given moment. You need to keep a clear head and be aware of your surroundings at all times. Be a smart traveler. There are websites to check for travel advisories and other important information. Usually, the country you are in will have websites for warnings as well. For the U.S., you can visit:

1. https://travel.state.gov/content/travel/en/travel advisories/traveladvisories.html/ Just put in the country you are wanting to travel to and see if there are any warnings.
2. https://www.usa.gov/travel-advisory Here you can sign up for STEP, The Smart Traveler Enrolment Program. When you enroll, you will receive emails with news, alerts, and travel advisories about your destination country.
3. https://wwwnc.cdc.gov/travel/notices CDC is good for keeping track of global health risks while

traveling. I honestly never thought about this prior to COVID. Now, I think about this a lot more! I think we all do.

I had friends who were in Morocco riding on camels in the desert when COVID hit and had no idea what was happening. I had other friends who were actually in Peru with a travel group in 2020. They paid a lot of money, $2,000 a month, to be a part of a country-hopping excursion. The point is that you have a group and a guide to take you through each country for a month. When the world shut down during COVID, they happened to be in Peru, and the company literally abandoned these travelers. Their guide left and went home to their own country. They left these Americans alone during a global pandemic in a foreign country. There were no domestic flights coming in and out. The company dismantled and vanished, and these people were on their own. I traveled with these people prior in 2019 in Asia. So, I messaged one of them to see if they were OK via Facebook messenger. I mean, what a horrifying experience!

He was a sixty-five-year-old male, world traveler, and pretty chill about the situation. But he was still stuck in Peru for two to three months. They were on lockdown and confined to their apartments as Peru instilled a military law during COVID. Men could only leave the house on Mondays, Wednesdays, and Fridays. Women could go out in public on Tuesdays, Thursdays, and Saturdays. No one left on Sundays. It was WAY stricter than the United States. There was a large military presence all around to keep the peace my friend said. It actually wasn't too bad by his accord, besides the fact that you couldn't go out and do anything other than to buy food and medicines. Since he was an American citizen, he had to wait until the U.S. sent planes over to extract our people from Peru. There were many Canadians there as well.

Apparently, they got back home to Canada quicker. He finally got back safely, and I think, other than being bored from confinement, he was OK. However, this also proves my point that even traveling abroad with a travel group doesn't protect you. If anything, it gives you a false sense of security. You always need to be a smart traveler no matter who you are with.

These photos are not from COVID, but from my trip. When we were in Cusco we stumbled upon a military parade.

Chapter 8 Food

One of my most favorite things to do: eat! I absolutely love eating and trying new foods in other regions. I think it's so much fun, and you learn a lot about a culture and its people by venturing out of your comfort zone and trying new foods. One of the cool things I discovered in Peru was the Asian influence on cuisine there, and I had no idea of its cultural significance. So much yummy Japanese food everywhere! If you are a Japanese food nut like me, it's hard to find the authentic stuff after you have actually lived in Japan and then come back to America. For example, ramen; I had the most amazing ramen in Kyoto back in 2019. It was mouthwatering, the type you write home to your mother about, dream about—that freaking good. My friend Jeff was also there with me, and we kept going back for more. Then we finally discovered why it was so rich and satisfying. They used lard in their broth. So very tasty indeed, but maybe not so much for the arteries! I was never able to find an amazing place in the States so far that even compared to the ramen in Kyoto. However, Peru did come close. But if you have ever had Japanese curry with chicken cutlet (also known as katsu curry), in Peru, they made it exactly the same. I have yet to even FIND a place in the United States that has Japanese curry. The next best place is in London. They make an excellent curry as well.

Katsu Curry

sushi

The other thing I learned while living in Peru for a month was they were actually the ones to invent ceviche; another favorite dish of mine. It's also considered the national dish of Peru. So, of course, I had to try some ceviche during my time there. It is a little bit different than what I was used to in the States. Most of the time, it came with cold, sweet potatoes, which was interesting. But it was always really good.

Ceviche is a cold dish. The fish or shellfish in ceviche is served raw; the citric acid from the citrus marinade causes the proteins in the seafood to become denatured, resulting in the dish appearing to be "cooked" without the application of heat. The fish is typically cured in lemon or sour lime juice, although sour orange was historically used. The dressing also includes some local variety of chili pepper or chili, replaced by mustard in some parts of Central

America. The marinade usually also includes sliced or chopped onions and chopped cilantro, though in some regions such as Mexico, tomatoes, avocadoes, and tomato sauce may be included. Ceviche is often eaten as an appetizer; if eaten as a main dish, it is usually accompanied by side dishes that complement its flavors, such as sweet potato, lettuce, maize, avocado, or fried plantains, among various other accompaniments.

The first documented evidence of the term ceviche is from 1820, in the patriotic song "La Chicha," considered the first Peruvian national anthem. It is recognized by UNESCO as an expression of Peruvian traditional cuisine and an Intangible Cultural Heritage of Humanity. (Wikipedia)

Ceviche with sweet potatoes, calamari, and green tea

Another popular meal in Peru that we stumbled upon was chicken, French fries, and this kind of purple punch. I guess it's not too far off from our beloved chicken fingers and fries here in the States. I swear, every day, another fast-food place pops up that only serves chicken fingers. Anyway, this version might've been a bit healthier? Nonetheless, it's a ton of food! Honestly, I think it was meant for four people, yet it was just the two of us. So, at this restaurant, all they serve is rotisserie-cooked, whole chicken breasts, French fries, and salad. Then, the condiments are mayo, mustard, dressing for the salad, and this purple-ish Kool-Aid. I'm not gonna knock it though because this meal was cheap and the perfect hangover cure. After we discovered this place, I seriously craved it. I mean it covered your basic four food groups: protein, vegetables, carbs, and purple glucose! Hahahaha.

The national drink of Peru is a pisco sour. It is a cocktail made with pisco, which is a grape brandy, and lime juice, sugar, and egg whites. It is a bit on the sour side, hence the name. Not a bad tasting drink, however. I'm not a huge sour person; I like sweet-tasting things more. But Jeff really liked them, so he often ordered them when we were out and about.

Although the preparation of pisco-based mixed beverages possibly dates back to the 1700s, historians and drink experts agree that the cocktail as it is known today was invented in the early 1920s in Lima, the capital of Peru, by the American bartender Victor Vaughen Morris. Morris left the United States in 1903 to work in Cerro de Pasco, a city in central Peru. In 1916, he opened

Morris' Bar in Lima, and his saloon quickly became a popular spot for the Peruvian upper class and English-speaking foreigners. The oldest known mentions of the pisco sour are found in newspaper and magazine advertisements, dating to the early 1920s, for Morris and his bar published in Peru and Chile. The pisco sour underwent several changes until Mario Bruiget, a Peruvian bartender working at Morris' Bar, created the modern Peruvian recipe for the cocktail in the latter part of the 1920s by adding Angostura bitters and egg whites to the mix.

The first grapevines were brought to Peru shortly after its conquest by Spain in the 16th century. Spanish chroniclers from the time note the first winemaking in South America took place in the hacienda Marcahuasi of Cuzco. The largest and most prominent vineyards of the 16th and 17th century Americas were established in the Ica valley of South-Central Peru. In the 1540s, Bartolomé de Terrazas and Francisco de Carabantes planted vineyards in Peru. Carabantes also established vineyards in Ica, where Spaniards from Andalucia and Extremadura introduced grapevines into Chile.

Already in the 16th century, Spanish settlers in Chile and Peru began producing aguardiente distilled from fermented grapes. Since at least 1764, Peruvian aguardiente was called "pisco" after its port of shipping; the usage of the name "pisco" for aguardiente then spread to Chile. The right to produce and market pisco, still made in Peru and Chile, is the subject of ongoing disputes between the two countries. (Wikipedia)

Chapter 9 Machu Picchu

When you are in Peru, you have to visit the iconic Machu Picchu. It was my entire reason for going to Peru in 2022. I wanted to hike and visit the beautiful mountain for my 45th birthday. It was a bucket list item for me, something I really wanted to accomplish as I am getting older. In 2019, while country hopping in Asia, we hiked the tallest mountain in Thailand which was exhausting and liberating all at the same time. I was with a group of mainly twenty-somethings, and I was the second oldest person, besides one other traveler who was in her fifties. We, of course, were at the back of the trail. However, we both did it! But I couldn't walk for four days afterwards, hahaha. My legs were so sore. The next morning, the entire group went out to breakfast, and I lied as to why I couldn't go. It's truthfully because I couldn't walk! OMG, it took me so long to recover. I was not in good shape prior to living in Asia for four months. But I lost over thirty pounds being in a healthier environment and eating cleaner foods. After that hike, it motivated me to start hiking more mountains. No, I was not going to age gracefully! I was going to conquer mountains all over the world and push myself to be the best version of myself.

So, I started training for Machu Picchu by climbing the stairs at the condo I lived in at the time. The building was fifteen stories high, and I would walk up and down the emergency staircase instead of taking the elevators. I used to do this in college when I went to school in Nebraska. Back then, I lived on the ninth floor. Stairs keep you in shape! Living in Florida, it's much harder when going to a higher altitude, so the problem I have now is getting used to the lack of oxygen. I should have bought some of those oxygen supplements; they advertise them all over Colorado. After getting my hiking bug, I started hiking more mountains in Colorado, North Carolina, and Georgia as well! In Peru, they make you acclimate to the higher elevation because it really is high in altitude. But first things first, you must book your entry. Here are my tips for making a smooth experience at Machu Picchu:

1. **Book Your Spot**

    If you want to visit this spot, you MUST book in advance! Book it as soon as they let you. I'm not kidding here. You can visit the website and see how far out you can book a spot. We stayed the entire month of September, my birth month, and didn't book it prior to leaving. We almost didn't get a spot! Thankfully, the first thing we did when landing in Peru was go to a travel agency and inquire. So, we had to do it like the last four days prior to the end of our trip. I was glad we actually got a spot. When we got to Cusco, there were tons of people waiting in long lines at other places who couldn't get in and were only there for a few days. If you are traveling for a week, book it in advance.

2. Use an Agency

Normally, I like to do things myself. And with the internet, most savvy people can. However, I would recommend using a travel agency on this one. Do you remember the old eighties movie, "Planes, Trains and Automobiles?" Yeah, to get to the mountain ... it's a lot like that. The number of things you must do and have perfectly timed so you don't miss your timeslot on the mountain is frankly insane. I'm a very organized person, and I had no idea what was going on, and I would have been lost if it wasn't for our multiple guides along the way meeting us, texting us, yelling at us, and telling us where to go. They coordinated *everything*. I mean, they coordinated the plane ride from Lima to Cusco, the hotel, the food, the car rides, the train, the bus ride, and the tour guide in Machu Picchu. And it only cost us $500 USD per person total for everything. That's a flipping deal.

3. Decide if You Want to Hike to Inca Trail or Take Transportation to Machu Picchu

So, there are a few different ways you can get to Machu Picchu. You could arrive the modern way, like I stated above via planes, trains, and automobiles. Alternatively, you could go the traditional route which is by walking the Inca Trail. This is how the Peruvian people did it back before modern transportation. If you are the more adventurous type, you might be up for this experience. However, you cannot do it on your own. You do have to book it with a guide and have a permit. The classic Inca Trail is twenty-six miles long and includes four days of hiking plus three days of camping. It would definitely be an experience, but as for me, I would be too exhausted once I got to Machu Picchu to enjoy it.

4. Buy Altitude Sickness Pills

Our flight from Miraflores to Cusco got in the day before we visited Machu Picchu. They give you a day to get used to the altitude. It's a very short flight, like 45 minutes out of Lima, so you basically have the entire day there. The change in altitude didn't really bother me as much as I thought it would; I just had to stop more to catch my breath when walking. However, it did make Jeff nauseous. Apparently, this is a bigger issue with younger people—win for getting older! They had tea in the hotel to drink to help with this, but you should buy some pills beforehand, just in case. We got them at a pharmacy in Miraflores.

5. Bring Snacks & Water

The day you go to Machu Picchu is going to be a very long one. Our company had a van pick us up at 6 AM. Since the hotel doesn't serve breakfast that early, they arranged for a to-go bag of snacks. Well, that wasn't nearly enough food for an entire day of hiking a huge mountain. I thought I was going to pass out because we didn't have   a real meal until like 4 PM that day. Our bagged food consisted of orange juice, a small banana, some weird bar of squishy nuts, and a few other small items. It was practically nothing; I mean, I would be hungry again by 9 AM on a normal day. There was no time to stop and get anything on the way either, not even water. I was so dehydrated.

6. Bring a Book to Read or Music to Listen to & a Remote Battery Charger for Your Phone

The time traveled from our hotel to the mountain was almost 6 hours long. If you get motion sickness, you might want to bring something for that too. Our van picked us up at 5 AM with another couple of ladies in Cusco. We drove for a few hours through windy, bumpy, narrow roads, through all kinds of small rural towns, which was kind of cool to see. Then we stopped at a train station where they gave us our tickets—we barely had enough time for a bathroom break!—and finally hopped on the train. The train ride was about another hour through the mountains which was absolutely beautiful. At this point, you can see the Inca Trail. You can see the people who are hiking their way to Machu Picchu with a guide. However, you will be spending a lot of time sitting and traveling to your destination, so bring things to occupy yourself. Plus, you want to save your batteries to take lots of amazing photos when you get to the mountains.

7. Pay Attention to Your Guides

Finally, you arrive in the town of Machu Picchu. This is where you get on a bus that takes you to the top of mountain where the entrance is. This part was super chaotic; there were so many people waiting for buses trying to get tickets. Thank goodness we already had ours, but we still had to have them issued from the station. The next guide grabbed and pushed us into the bus station to get our tickets, then put us at the back of one line. There were so many lines, it was so confusing, everyone was yelling in Spanish, and it was hot. Then I realized it was noontime, and our entry time into the park was stamped for 1 PM. I was like, are we going to make it? We told our guide this and then he grabbed us and we all started running. We passed up all these people and buses and then he pushed us to the front of the line and got us on the very next bus leaving. We cut in front of all these people! He said something very quickly in Spanish to the bus driver then waived us on in front of other angry tourists. Boom—we were off! If it was just us trying to figure that out on our own, we would still be waiting at the back of the bus, hahaha. Again, it really does pay to be part of a tour group that knows what is going on and the people who work there.

8. Wear Hiking Shoes & Comfortable Clothing in Layers

Now, we were on our bus with about forty other people, starting the windy road up the hill to the top of the gates toward the entrance of Machu Picchu. It was a very narrow, windy road with other buses coming down as well, which was kind of scary, honestly, because it was so steep. People were walking up this road too, but again, it is steep and narrow, so you had to dodge the buses. Personally, I preferred the bus with AC. It was hot. The temp in Cusco was totally different than the temp in the mountains; it was literally twenty-some degrees hotter in the city of Machu Picchu. Here, I wore leggings with a short-sleeved, thin shirt, a rain jacket—because it literally calls for rain every day there—and my hiking boots. I was cold when I left Cusco, but then I was hot when we arrived four hours later, so I just put my jacket in my backpack. You also cannot bring hiking sticks or selfie sticks in the park, but honestly, you really don't need them. You will be walking through narrow parts of the ruins with lots of people so there is no room for one. Overall, it's not a bad hike. Just a bit of a hill to the top, then the main part, which was fairly flat.

9. Tour Guides

Once we got to the top, there were really long lines to get into the site. We met our guide outside the archeological site. I normally don't do things like this with a guide, but it was actually really helpful. For one, the site was included with everything else. Two, he was very knowledgeable about the history. And three, he took tons of photos of us on site. Honestly, that was the best part; it was like having our own photographer who knew all the best shots. You don't need a selfie stick because they will take the best photos for you!

10. Two Additional Areas to Hike

There are two additional mountains you can hike once you are at the Machu Picchu site. They are much taller mountains, and you need an additional permit to go. Huayna Picchu and Machu Picchu Mountain are two mountains on opposite sides of the Machu Picchu archeological site, which are possible to hike to enjoy panoramic views from the top. Huayna Picchu is the tall peak you see in most photos of Machu Picchu, while Machu Picchu Mountain is located at the opposite end of the site. Huayna Picchu is steeper, and there are some parts where you need to use your hands for balance. Machu Picchu Mountain is not as steep, but the elevation gain is double that of Huayna Picchu. It is also a longer hike making it a bit more physically challenging overall. It contains a narrow staircase rightfully called the stairs of death. Jeff wanted to do this, and I looked up at it with a bad gut feeling before even asking our guide. He responded that at least one person falls and dies on that hike every year. The park and the Peruvian government make you sign a death waiver before you get your permit. I'm assuming the verbiage says something about you or your next of kin not suing or making a big stink about you dying on the stairs of death, because they warned you! So, that was a big NOPE from me. I want to do cool shit on my bucket list, but I would also like to be alive in order to write books about it to share with the world after the fact.

11. Weather

The weather at the end of September was honestly absolutely gorgeous. It was cooler in Miraflores by the ocean, but it was a warm, beautiful, sunny day at the top of the mountain. If I ever go back, I would for certain go again during this time frame. It would stink to hike in the rain. Not only would it be hard to see anything, but it would also be slippery and muddy. They had plastic grates all over the ground in case of rain to prevent mudslides, etc. But it wouldn't be fun at all. I can imagine it's similar to the tropical downpour of Florida since you are all the way out in the middle of the jungle. So, definitely avoid it during the rainy season of January, February, and March.

12. Time

It took about two hours to walk around all the ruins in the main areas of the site. The day is a very long one, yet you only spend a few hours inside. But it was totally worth it to step back in time. Machu Picchu was a fairly recent archeological discovery, our guide told us. It was abandoned by the Inca people back in the early 1500's as they were worried the Spanish conquistadors would find it, but they never did. It became overgrown with foliage and hidden to the outside world until 1911 and was then rediscovered by an American explorer called Hiram Bingham.

13. Stamp in Your Passport

After you are done hiking at the site, you then take the bus back down the windy road to the actual city of Machu Picchu. We had a few hours to kill before we go on our train and started the four-hour trek back to Cusco. By this time, I was starving! It was around 3 PM—the last thing I ate was at 6 AM, so again, pack snacks. Thankfully, there were many restaurants in town to grab some food at. We scarfed down food then walked around and found another long line of people in the middle of the city center. We discovered there they will stamp your passport with Machu Picchu! How cool is that? So of course, we had to. I love collecting passport stamps. Bring yours if you want to stamp it, to officially have it on paper that you hiked a World Heritage Site.

Peru Rail: the train we took.

The City Center of Machu Picchu where you can get the stamp.

At the top of Machu Picchu!

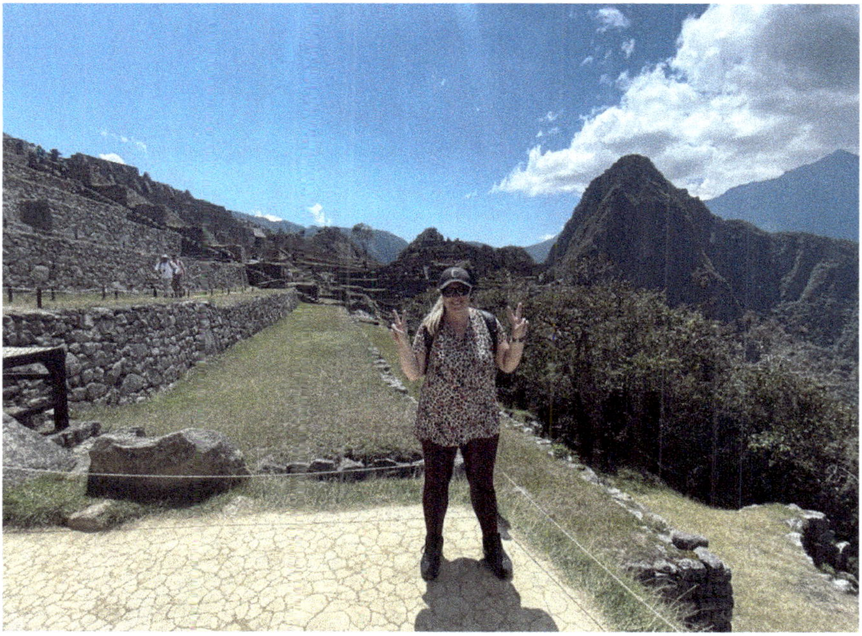

GESTION 2015-2018
MACHUPICCHU
Ciudad del Mundo

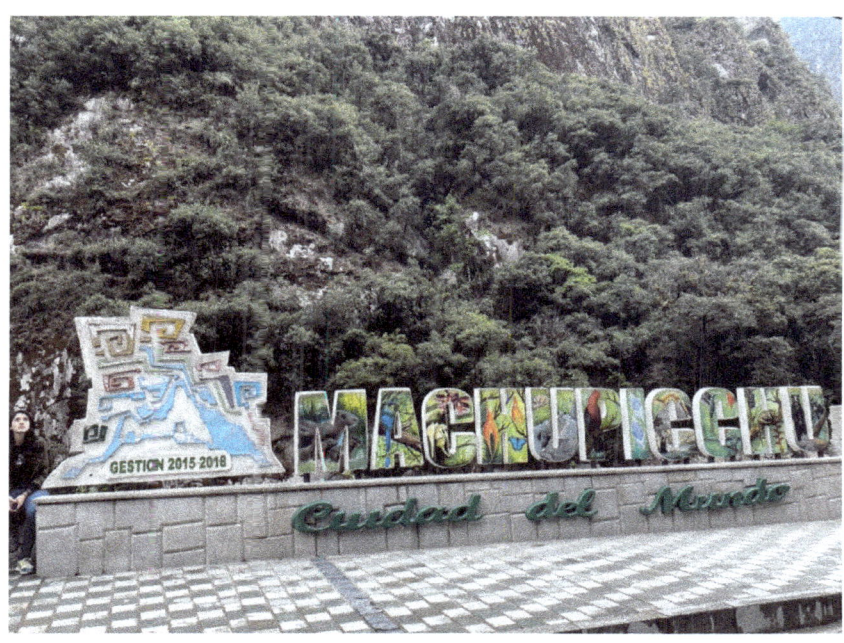

Chapter 10 Working Remotely

I guess we have to work sometime, right? It cannot all be just fun and games and hanging out with the llamas in Peru. But being a digital nomad at least has the perks and the freedom to do all the fun things you want to when you are not working. I am an entrepreneur and own my own indie publishing house, plus I also do real estate, so this gave me a bit more flexibility within my schedule. Jeff, my travel buddy, actually has a full-time job and worked for a company while we were in Peru. So, his schedule was a bit more regimented. However, he is 100% remote, so he just had to work around the time zone differences and meetings etc. Even though he is a remote worker anyway, he still told his manager that he would be in another country for the month of September. I think this would be a good move for anyone who already has a remote job. Communication, above all, is the best

thing you can have in any relationship, especially in a work environment. I mean, if you have to do a Zoom meeting and they see mountains in the background when you normally live in Florida, they might know something is up! The good thing about Peru is the time zone is not that much different than in the states. It is one hour behind Florida, so for me, it was perfect to attend calls and meetings. Jeff's company was based out of California, so not too far off there either. Time zone differences are a big thing to factor in when you are looking at places to go to work remotely. I met Jeff back in 2019 when we were country-hopping through Asia for four months. That was a much more difficult time zone to manage. I remember having to be stuck at my apartment doing client calls at 8 PM while everyone else was out having fun because that was like 8 AM the next day back in Florida. That really sucked, and it was actually the entire reason I took away free phone consults on my website.

I learned so many life lessons while country-hopping in Asia, but a big one was that my time definitely is worth more than money. There I was in Vietnam, having a once-in-a-lifetime experience, yet I am stuck every night on the phone with people who are just wanting free publishing advice and most likely not going to sign up for my services. Am I going to give away all of my precious energy instead of going out there and experiencing what the beautiful city of Hanoi had to offer? Hell no! That is the beauty of being a digital nomad. I was able to streamline my work time down to a few hours a day, cut out the unnecessary stuff that was wasting time and energy so the time I did spend working was only to maximize profits. I then realized 80% of the stuff I did was just nonsense. Only 20% of my tasks were actually making money. Then I inserted a grueling weeding out process for new authors. I made them jump through hoops. They had to earn my time because otherwise I was going to be outside meditating with the monks or hiking a mountain.

Here are some tips for working in Peru:

1. **Wi-Fi:** The Wi-Fi in Peru is pretty good. We never had any issues. You could get one of those hotspot modules, but I don't think you would need it. There was always a strong signal in our Airbnb, and I had to upload large files for

publishing, so I never had any issues with uploads or downloads.
2. **Coffee Shops:** Jeff and I usually ended up just working from our apartment we rented for the month. It was a nice two-story place on the beachside. I flipped-flopped from the couch to outside to get some fresh air. He liked sitting in the kitchen. In Peru, there didn't seem to be lots of internet cafes or coffee shops to work from like in Thailand or Vietnam. When we were in Asia, I would always go out for a morning walk and take my laptop to get some yummy eggs, coffee, and hang out in a super cute café to work. They were loaded with them there. But not so much in Peru. I mean, they have Starbucks, but I'm in Peru. I don't want to spend my time at the bucks. I guess it's because Thailand has been the number one expat place for a long time. If you build it, they will come.
3. **Coworking Spots:** Not many of those here either. I suppose because we were in Miraflores. We found one close by, but it was expensive and not that great. We tried it out and barely stayed for one hour. It was really hard to find and even harder for the receptionist to understand why we were even there, LOL. There was a bigger coworking space by the big mall they have which is called Larcomar. They have pretty much all the modern shops and restaurants you need there! It's an upscale area. It was walking distance from our place; it took about twenty minutes to walk there, or less in a short Uber ride.
https://www.larcomar.com

Picture of the mall from their website

Managing your time effectively as a digital nomad is crucial for maintaining productivity and achieving a healthy work-life balance. What Jeff and I would do is plan out our week ahead of time. We decided what fun stuff we wanted to do and where we wanted to explore that week in Peru, then what was on our work plate, carving out our free time in between meetings and tasks we had to accomplish. He always had morning meetings, so I knew I could get in a few hours of work between 8 AM to noon. Then we would either go out for a walk for lunch or order some food in. FYI, they have tons more options in Peru than just Uber Eats, and it's way cheaper too! I never do food delivery in the States unless it's pizza because the prices are crazy insane, but in Peru the delivery fees are like 2 USD, so we ordered lots of food! If we didn't have meetings during the afternoons, then we would go off on adventures. Sometimes, he would actually take some vacation days like when we were in Cusco to hike Machu Picchu just because he didn't want to have to be stuck in a meeting. Also, we discovered the Wi-Fi in the hotel there was crappy, so working from that particular place would not have been easy.

Here are some strategies to help you manage your time:

1. **Set Clear Goals**: Define your short-term and long-term goals for both work and personal time. This will help you stay focused and track your progress.
2. **Create a Daily Schedule**: Establish a routine that outlines your work hours, breaks, and personal activities. Consistent scheduling can improve productivity and time management.
3. **Use Time Management Tools**: Utilize apps and tools like Trello, Asana, or Todoist for task management and calendar apps for scheduling. These tools can help you stay organized and prioritize tasks.
4. **Prioritize Tasks**: Use methods like the Eisenhower Matrix to identify urgent and important tasks. Focus on high-priority items first to ensure that critical work gets done.
5. **Time Blocking**: Allocate specific blocks of time for different tasks or projects. This minimizes distractions and helps you stay committed to focused work.
6. **Limit Distractions**: Identify and minimize distractions in your environment. This could mean finding a quiet workspace or using apps that block distracting websites.
7. **Set Boundaries**: Clearly define when you are working and when you are off work. Communicate these boundaries to friends and family to reduce interruptions.
8. **Incorporate Breaks**: Schedule regular breaks to recharge, whether it's a short walk, exercise, or a coffee break. This can enhance focus and prevent burnout.

9. **Embrace Flexibility**: One of the advantages of being a digital nomad is flexibility. Be open to adjusting your schedule to fit local activities or opportunities.
10. **Assess and Reflect**: Regularly review your schedule and productivity. Assess what is working and what isn't and make adjustments as needed to improve efficiency.

By applying these strategies, you can effectively manage your time while enjoying the freedom and experiences that come with being a digital nomad. Even though you are traveling, you still have to keep a schedule. Some people think that by being a digital nomad, you are just "on vacation." This is the farthest thing from the truth. In order to be a "successful nomad," you have to be very disciplined. Some people cannot balance the two.

What Not to Do as a Digital Nomad

I have been traveling the world extensively since I could walk. I have always had a curiosity for travel and exploring other countries and cultures, way before the term "digital nomad" was a thing. I have also been an entrepreneur. Yes, I did have nine-to-five jobs throughout my lifetime but ingrained in my soul path was always to run my own businesses. The publishing house was not even my first successful one. Before Richter Publishing LLC, I had a computer repair business that I ran for five years that did well. Prior to that, I had multiple eBay stores. Even currently, I sell stuff on Etsy. Once an entrepreneur, always an entrepreneur.

The biggest mistake I see digital nomads making is they want the lifestyle, but they do not know how to get a job that supports it. They just want the freedom to travel but have no idea how to do it. They quit their job, move to Thailand or Peru FIRST, then try to get a remote job once they are in another country. **NO!** A thousand times nooooooooo! Then they run out of money and end up becoming backpack beggars. That is an official term I learned while living in Thailand for two months. I'll let you in on a little secret: other countries' governments hate this. They will not support you and will kick you out of their country. Countries do like expats, but they only want expats with *money*.

Technically, you are not supposed to be legally working in another country unless you have a work visa. However, when it's remote work, it is usually not a big deal because the company you are working for is located somewhere else. Thailand, for example, is very strict on this as they do not want backpack beggars taking away jobs from their local people. Makes sense right? So, the only jobs that an English-speaking person can get, with a proper work visa, is teaching English in the school system to Thai children. That was the job all the expats I knew that lived in Thailand long term actually had. But wait... that is not the digital nomad dream. Is it? Not for me it's not. Now, you are stuck in a regular 9-5 job, now you get paid a salary, and that salary is in Thai Baht. Now, you have to work to pay your rent and bills—what happened to your freedom?! **NO!** The digital nomad dream is to make American money remotely and then live in a place where your USD is converted from $1 to 33.83 Thai Baht, and you dictate your own schedule!

I am in multiple Facebook expat groups all over the world. I actually recommend joining them for the country you will be visiting for tips, tricks, etc. But it blows my mind the number of nomads that are in there asking for jobs that are already living in a foreign country and don't have a job. Like, how did you really expect this to work? You think it will be easier for you to get a job in another country as a foreign entity? Do you see what is going on in America right now in 2025? They are deporting people at a massive rate. No, it will not be easier for you to just go somewhere else and get a job. Especially a remote work one. You need to have the infrastructure set up already before you leave. Either you own a business that is stable or have been at a job for a while that will allow the remote work from another country. I have owned and operated the publishing house for about twelve years now, since 2013. However, the first five years I was hustling my ass off to build and grow it. No way I could just hop on a plane and live in Peru. I was working fifteen-hour days killing myself. Since I put in that blood, sweat, and tears, now my company is fairly self-running, and I can work from anywhere in the world. But not in the beginning. So, before you make the leap, think first if it's the right move for you.

After my first divorce, I moved to Palm Harbor, lived in a condo, and got a roommate to share expenses with at the age of thirty-two. This lady who answered my ad was in her early fifties and worked for Delta's call center. She had worked there for twenty-some years and loved the benefits of free flights. She was a party animal and enjoyed live concerts. Since she had seniority at the call center, they gave her the option of working from home. But she never took it. Instead, she commuted an hour in traffic from Palm Harbor to Tampa twice a day. I asked her, "Why?" We lived in a gorgeous community by the Innisbrook golf course. I, of course, worked from home, as I always have. Instead of spending two hours a day sitting in that horrible traffic, I would go to our gym, sit by the pool, sleep in—anything besides Tampa traffic! This was her response: "I cannot work from home, because if I did, I would be drunk by noon at the pool and get nothing done."

WOW!

I mean, at least she was honest with herself. I knew she liked to drink—a lot—but I didn't know she had zero control over it. So, the decision to be a digital nomad isn't a light one. Do you have what it takes? Do you have the discipline to be in an amazing new country with temptations all around you and be able to balance fun with tasks? I guess I have always had a Type A personality, so I have to accomplish something first before I can reward myself. However, I do think the main key to working remotely and being successful at it is *organization,* by carving out the work time and the fun time. If you can balance the two and stick to it, the world can be your oyster!

Working from our balcony in Miraflores

Chapter 11 Rainbow Mountain

Rainbow Mountain, or Vinicunca, is a stunning natural landmark located in the Andes of Peru, near the city of Cusco. It is another iconic tourist destination, especially if you are looking for that great shot for the gram. We did not make it to Rainbow Mountain. I was not aware of it until we arrived in Peru. After doing research, it did seem that it was a more strenuous hike, and I was saving my hiking legs for Machu Picchu.

Here are some key points about Rainbow Mountain:

1. **Unique Geology**: The mountain gets its vibrant colors from the mineral deposits that are present in the soil, including red, yellow, green, and blue hues. This unique geological phenomenon creates an awe-inspiring visual spectacle.
2. **Accessibility**: Rainbow Mountain is typically accessed through trekking tours organized from Cusco. The hike to the summit can be challenging due to high altitude

(over 5,200 meters or around 17,060 feet—that's almost half the height of Mount Everest!) and varying weather conditions.
3. **Best Time to Visit**: The best time to visit is during the dry season, from May to September. However, it's still possible to visit during other months, although weather conditions may vary.
4. **Cultural Significance**: The area around Rainbow Mountain is home to Indigenous communities, and the mountain is often associated with local folklore and cultural beliefs.
5. **Preparation**: For those planning to hike to Rainbow Mountain, it's essential to acclimatize to the altitude, stay hydrated, and prepare for changing weather conditions. Layered, warm clothing and sturdy footwear are recommended. Bring an oxygen tank just in case because of the extreme altitude. Not all tour companies will have them on hand.
6. **Photography**: The vibrant colors and breathtaking landscapes make Rainbow Mountain a popular spot for photography, drawing tourists from around the world.
7. **Preservation Efforts**: Due to its popularity, there have been efforts to manage tourism and minimize environmental impact. Visitors are encouraged to respect nature and local customs.

Visiting Rainbow Mountain provides not only stunning views but also opportunities to connect with the natural beauty and cultural richness of Peru. Tours usually start early like 3 AM if you want to beat the crowds to get better photos. It's going to be a long journey to the mountain as well, as it's a three-hour drive from Cusco. The actual hike is about three to four hours long. However, it seems they do have an option to ride a horse through some of the flatter sections of the trek.

Photo from https://www.rainbowmountainperu.com/rainbow-mountain-trek/

Chapter 12 Sand Dunes & Sea Lions

A large portion of Peru's coastline is part of the Sechura Desert, which is part of the larger Atacama Desert system, one of the driest places on Earth. The desert's arid conditions prevent vegetation growth, allowing wind to freely shape the loose sand into dunes. Strong coastal winds carry fine sand particles and deposit them over time, creating large dunes. Wind patterns constantly shift and reshape the dunes, making them dynamic in form. I had no idea Peru had a desert. It was really breathtaking to see in person. I literally felt like I had taken a plane ride to an entirely different country and landed in the middle of the Sahara.

We did a day excursion and went sandboarding at the Huacachina Dunes. Huacachina is such a cool spot—a literal oasis in the desert. You'll get to see massive dunes surrounding a lagoon and the amazing sunset views. It was another long trip that also included a boat ride at the beach town called Paracas, which is roughly an hour and a half-hour drive from Huacachina. Paracas is famous for its Paracas National Reserve, where you can see dramatic desert-meets-ocean landscapes, red sand beaches, and plenty of wildlife, including sea lions and flamingos.

We booked this excursion through an online tour group that Jeff found. It was definitely a fun experience and something different that I was not expecting at all to do in Peru. I will break it down for you how our trip went. I do not remember the exact name of the tour that we booked, but there are multiple ones you will find:

1. **Early:** Again, this tour is going to go early in the a.m. because Paracas is about a four-hour drive from Lima. We were staying in Miraflores. The nice thing about this tour was that they picked us up from our Airbnb. A small van came to our place around five am to get us and then drop us off at another location in Lima where we waited for the big bus to come. Now, they were not very good at communicating this info. We didn't know we were taking multiple vehicles in the pitch-black darkness in unidentified vans. We asked questions, we got no responses. When the driver pulled up and shoved us out to a closed coffee shop and then quickly left, it was a tad unnerving. For about fifteen minutes I thought, possibly, Jeff had sold us into some underground sex trafficking ring. Thankfully, a guide came soon who spoke English and told us what was going on.
2. **Bus Ride:** Once everyone else arrived safely, we all piled onto a big bus and headed to Paracas. Again, bring snacks and/or headphones, backup battery charger for your phones, etc. Bring something to do on the bus. Maybe a pillow to go back to sleep. It was a long, boring ride. I think they did give us water and some small protein bar.
3. **Paracas:** Once we arrived at the beach town, we all went to a restaurant and had time to buy breakfast. So that was nice because we arrived around 10 a.m. We took a bathroom break, too, because the one on the bus didn't

work. The town was really cute and had little shops, etc. Here's our breakfast, simple but did the job!

4. **Boat Ride:** After our refreshing little breakfast, we then all loaded onto a boat from the pier behind the boardwalk shown in the photo above. We took about an hour ride out to see the famous Candelabra landmark, sea lions, and the Ballestas Islands.

5. **Candelabra:** The Candelabra of Paracas (El Candelabro de Paracas) is a massive geoglyph etched into a sandy hillside on the Paracas Peninsula, overlooking the Pacific Ocean. It's one of Peru's most famous and mysterious landmarks. It measures around 595 feet tall and 210 feet wide, making it visible from several miles away at sea. The shape resembles a three-pronged candelabrum, though some speculate it may represent a cactus or a trident. The geoglyph is estimated to be around 2,000–2,500 years old, dating back to the Paracas culture (roughly 200 BCE). Some believe it was used as a landmark for sailors, guiding them along the coast. Others believe it was created by aliens, similar to the crop circles in corn fields! Crazy that it is still there after all these years.

6. **Sea Lions:** You will see lots of sea lions chilling on new and old boats on the trip. There are penguins too, but we didn't see as many penguins. Here are a bunch of sea lions hanging out on the front of this big commercial ship. Apparently, they are all female besides the big guy in the back. He's big poppa.

7. **Bird Poop Paradise AKA Ballestas Islands**: The next stop you might want to bring nose plugs. OMG. I can still smell these photos years later. The reason for the massive amount of bird droppings, guano, is due to the huge seabird population that nests there year-round. These birds produce tons of guano as they feast on the abundant fish in the surrounding waters. There is a variety of birds that live on the islands: Peruvian boobies, Guanay cormorant, and pelicans. The Humboldt Current brings nutrient-rich waters to the region, attracting massive schools of fish. The birds have a steady food supply, leading to large, stable colonies and, of course, lots of poop. The islands are much bigger than the photo I have here. We circled around them as the guide told us the stories of "white gold." I, in the meantime, was about ready to pass out from the stench.

8. **White Gold**: In the 19th century, guano was a highly valued fertilizer, and Peru's guano deposits were heavily mined. The Ballestas Islands were part of this "Guano Boom," with workers harvesting the bird droppings for export. Guano became a highly valuable commodity because it was an excellent natural fertilizer. Guano is packed with essential nutrients for farming: nitrogen (N) which boosts plant growth, phosphorus (P) which strengthens roots, and potassium (K) which improves disease resistance. Between 1840 and 1870, Peru became one of the world's largest guano exporters, making it incredibly wealthy. Countries like Britain, France, and the United States imported massive amounts of guano from Peru. Guano profits were used to fund infrastructure and pay off national debts. Hence, the name white gold was coined. Who knew poop was profitable?!

9. **Sand Dunes:** After our boat adventure, we loaded back onto the bus and started the one hour and fifteen-minute drive to Huacachina. I would advise wearing tennis shoes during the sand dune adventure. I didn't know this, and the guides didn't tell us in advance. I wore flip-flops because I'm a Florida girl, and I always wear them. However, trying to hike up a huge sand dune is a totally different experience versus walking on a flat beach. They kept falling off my feet in the slippery sand, so I just took them off. Holy smokes Batman! I thought I got a third-degree burn on the bottom of my feet. This is not the same sand back at Clearwater beach. I can walk barefoot there but not here, nope! So, I put my flip-flops back on, but the sand would seep in as my feet sunk, and it still burned my toes! UGH! I don't think I have to mention it was blazing hot besides the sand. The temp differences we experienced on this trip were extreme. From cold in the a.m. in Lima, to chilly on the boat in Paracas, to my face and feet with third-degree sunburns in Huacachina. Sunscreen? Yes, bring some. I ended up buying a hat at the oasis shops because I was literally getting a sunburn on my forehead.

10. **Dune Buggy Ride:** If you like crazy adventures, this one is for you. To get to the sandboarding area, you will take a dune buggy to get there. I might be naïve, but I had no idea what I was getting myself into. I didn't realize it was going to be a "chasing the bad guy in a 007 movie scene, and we were the crash test dummies in the back." This buggy drove over these dunes at what felt like a hundred miles an hour launching us into the sand. I was in the very back and bounced around like a rag doll! My head kept crashing into the ceiling, and I have no idea how I held

onto my GoPro to film it at all, but it did bend the stick. Tip: sit in the front or middle seat; it's not as bumpy as the back. On the way back, this polite Canadian couple let us ride in the middle. Halfway through she's yelling that he is driving faster this time. Hahaha, nope! It just feels much worse in the backseat! This ride is not for the faint of heart or anyone who has neck or back issues. Overall, it was fun, but I seriously thought at one point we were gonna flip over. You were warned, LOL.

Chapter 13 Manicures & Pedicures in Peru

This was a very interesting experience I had in Peru, to say the least. I have had manicures and pedicures in other parts of the world, but I would say this experience definitely takes the cake. Manis & pedis in other parts of the world are different from America, which is to be expected. When I lived in Asia for four months, I never got a decent pedicure. They just don't do them like we do back in the States. Thai nail salons have the exact same chairs that we do in America, the massage ones with the water basin to soak your feet. But with my experiences, they never actually filled it with water and did not do the entire pedicure experience of soaking your feet, cutting the cuticles, getting in and cutting out the ingrown toenails, scrubbing off your callouses. Everything that we are used to getting in America. In Thailand, basically, they just changed the nail polish, cut down the nails, and filed them a little bit. Same with your hands. They only used regular nail polish too, no gel. If you had acrylics, forget about it. You are in trouble. I have real nails, but I use gel on them. That stuff is hard to get off. They use a tool, kinda like a drill bit. They file it down and then put acetone on it and soak it, then file it off. After living in Thailand for 4 months and not getting a proper pedicure, my ingrown toenails were so bad I could barely walk. I didn't realize what an amazing job my nail tech did back home. Or I guess how bad my toes would get because I usually get one at least every two months. In the States, nail techs have to be certified and have a license. So, they are trained; in other countries, I have no idea.

Let's get back to my pedicure in Peru. I was staying in a 5-star hotel to research for a writing retreat I was planning. I figure this is as good a place as any to get a mani-pedi, right? I didn't have time before I left FL because I was running around like a chicken with my head cut off getting ready for my trip. My nails grow really fast. So, I figured I will just do it when I get to Peru. Well, here I am two weeks into the trip and still haven't done it. And my nails are super long.   book the appointment, and I am excited because I really need this.

I arrive at the spa in the hotel right on time. The receptionist says the masseuse is running behind, and I can hang out in the sauna for 10 -15 minutes. Ok cool, but I'm confused. I booked a mani pedi? She takes me into the lockers and tells me to change into a robe. Um ok, but why am I taking off my clothes for a manicure? I comply so I can go to the sauna since I have on velour sweats and a sweatshirt. I go in the sauna, and she says I can leave the bathrobe outside. Um no... I didn't dress for this I came for a manicure... I'm naked under this! I sit in the sauna in my bathrobe and enjoy the hot coals for about 5-7 minutes. It is a nice change from the chilly weather outside in Miraflores' winter months. Before this, I have been staying at an Airbnb without heat. So, this is awesome. Did I mention the hotel has heat in the hallways? However, I get a little too warm, and I decide to exit the sauna and go back and put my clothes on to get ready for my mani pedi because I assume I will be sitting in a chair like every other mani pedi I've had in 45 years on this planet.

I leave and tell the receptionist I'm going to change, and she looks at me weird. But I'm putting my pants back on because this robe will show off my girly bits, and I need to be properly clothed for this. After I am clothed, they take me into the room, and it's a massage room. And I said I booked a mani pedi, and they said yes. Um ok... Where's the chair? There's two ladies in there already that only speak Spanish. The receptionist speaks English and is translating. My Spanglish is so-so, even after being married to a Nicaraguan for four years and taking it in high school. I really should be better. But with all the face masks, it makes it hard for me. I have to read lips, and it makes it much harder to understand under the mask since I'm very rusty to begin with.

They ask me what color I want and lay down the OPI colors on the bed. I choose a dark red. They only had 8 to choose from. I really wanted black but red it is. Then she asked how far to cut them down etc., shape of nail, normal questions, then she exited the room. And I hopped up on the massage table, and they started working on taking off the nail polish I already had on. This was just kinda bizarre because you are laying down, only half propped up and can't really see what they are doing. I've had my nails done in a spa before in the States, and they never did it like this, but we are in Peru. So, I was like let's just enjoy it. And I was for a moment.

I kinda dozed off because what else are you going to do laying there on a bed? I had gel on my hands but not on my feet. However, since this isn't a nail salon, they didn't have the proper tools to take it off. And I wasn't paying attention. All I felt was this scrapping and yanking motion on my hands. And I'm thinking they need the grinder tool. But I guess they know what they are doing right? WRONG. All of a sudden, PAIN shot up my pinky finger, and I screamed out as she scraped so hard she ripped my nail off the nailbed, all the way down into the meaty part because they were scrapping the gel off and didn't soak it at all in acetone. I looked at my nails, and they are just mutilated. I'm horrified. It looked like I got attacked by an animal.

"WHAT ARE YOU DOING?!" I yelled. This is not how you take off gel. They had scrapped and ruined my nailbeds to where there were practically no nails left. Because my nails were so long, they were trying to pull the gel off the ends and were just ripping them. The assistant went out to find the lady that spoke English. It took a while, so she must have been on break. During that time, I told the other lady to give me the nail file. I told her this is how you take off gel. You have to buff it down first. And I started doing my own nails. I buffed them, got them coarse, then we put the acetone on with the wraps to let it soak so we can file it off later. By the time we finished doing it properly together, the English-speaking lady was back.

I explained to her what happened, the lady still in the room blamed what happened on the assistant, but honestly, neither one of them knew what they were doing. And my poor pinky was broken badly, now burning with acetone on it. So, she kept working on my toes. Then 10 minutes later, a more senior lady came in, and she then started working on my hands. I was super nervous, and now I'm paying attention. She took off the first wrap, and the other girl tossed the scrapping tool towards her, and she ignored it. She got a nail file and started filing off the gel.

I sighed with relief. Thank god, someone knows what they are doing here.

She cut my nails and filed them and even was able to fix my pinky finger. She had the other lady go out and buy superglue. She was top notch. So glad they sent her in. I could finally relax and get my mani-pedi after all. Hopefully, it will stay together long enough to grow out and heal.

It was over two hours already. The other girl left, all my nails are painted, and I'm like ok we have to be done here. I'm over this I really just want to go back to my hotel room. Then the lady put cucumbers on my eyes, and I'm like oh what's this? She takes my hand and does like a hand massage thing, which they will do sometimes at a nail salon, but then she swings my arm over my head, to the back and switches a lever under me. I hear a BOOM, and I'm down flat in the massage bed. I'm like OMG is this the happy ending ... what is happening. Then she starts stretching my arms and legs and doing a full-on body massage.

I can't see anything; I still don't know what's going on. I'm glad I have on my face mask because I can't help but laugh. I'm thinking, is she going to ask me to flip over? Am I getting a back massage? No, my nails are wet. I'm so confused. I have no idea what is happening right now. Then she's just like, "Ok, we done!"

This is hands down the weirdest mani-pedi I have ever had in my life. But in the end, my nails turned out ok. They didn't charge me for the mani since they mutilated my pinky and only charged me for the pedi and that unusual happy ending which came to a whopping $36. Would I do it again? Not sure....

There may be other nail salons that do gel manicures in Peru in better places. Jeff and I went out for drinks in a popular area called Kennedy Park. Now I'm obsessed with checking out local ladies' nails. Because I just can't believe in a city like San Isidro, where you can see people driving expensive cars like Porsches, they don't have decent manicures. The bar we popped into had a nail salon next to it, and I peered in the window--it looked more like our salons back in the States. My pinky finger throbbed with jealousy that those women were most likely getting a decent manicure. A good tip would be before you venture into this service in another country, make sure they know the type of polish you have and or service they can or cannot do first. Save your fingers the heartache!

Chapter 14 Travel Insurance and Hurricanes

The month of September went by fast and soon our trip and living in Peru was soon to come to an end. I had an amazing time being a digital nomad and exploring all that Peru had to offer despite some of the things we encountered, but that it all part of the adventure, right? Well, I guess the universe heard my plea to stay in Peru because the day that Jeff and I were set to leave and go back to the states, hurricane Ian blew through Florida.

Hurricane Ian made landfall in Florida on September 28, 2022. The first landfall occurred at 3:05 p.m. EDT on Cayo Costa, a barrier island in southwestern Florida, with maximum sustained winds of 150 mph (240 km/h), classifying it as a high-end Category 4 hurricane. Approximately an hour and a half later, at 4:35 p.m. EDT, Ian made a second landfall near Punta Gorda, Florida, with estimated sustained winds of 145 mph (235 km/h). (Source: National Hurricane Center)

So, for a little background on me. I think my birthday might be cursed. I was born on 9-11-77. Many bad things have happened on my birthday. I don't think I need to explain the most horrific thing of them all and why everyone gives a big sigh when I hand over my driver's license and they see 9-11. However, I keep having bad luck on my birthday. The year I came back from country-hopping in Asia, it was my birthday, and I decided to have an Asian inspired party. I wanted to share all the amazing food I ate living in Vietnam, Japan, Thailand and Singapore with my friends and family. One of my authors is a chef so I asked him to cater it. Well, that went horribly wrong. I rented out the clubhouse in my condo complex and he and his sous chef simultaneously almost burned down my condo along with the kitchen in the clubhouse. I really didn't think cooking rice was that hard, but as my guests were putting out flames on his hibachi grill in the party room, I went back to my condo to find my cat choking to death on black fumes because they left food burning in my own kitchen on the stove. To this day, I have no idea how none of the fire alarms went off or how the building didn't get swarmed by firetrucks.

On my 40th birthday, I rented out a gulf front suite on St. Pete Beach with professional photographers, catered food, cake, and all the festivities for my friends to celebrate. Instead, hurricane Irma decided to make an appearance. My birthday was again destroyed. Irma's impact was extensive, causing severe damage across the state. I spent my birthday hunkered down with my dad and cat inside my condo listening to the howling winds outside, instead of the magnificent party I had planned.

I don't have good luck with my birthday MONTH. Let alone the day. So, this year, 2022, I decided why don't I just leave the country? It seems hurricanes are going to ruin it, so what if I just leave for the entire month, good right? LOL NO. Destiny had other plans. Funny enough Jeff and I went out on my actual birthday to a restaurant in Branco and I ended up with food poisoning! He was fine…. seriously. However, I thought I had avoided the hurricane fiasco. Until I went to go back to Florida.

Jeff and I were checking into our flights and my layover out of Panama was canceled due to weather. I didn't even know there was a hurricane brewing out there. We were not watching the news. So, I had no clue. His flights were fine because he was going back to Colorado, mine were not, as the entire state of Florida was closed for business. The crap thing was there was no one to talk to about it. The airline was not canceling my first flight out of Peru because that one was fine, but the second leg was already canceled days in advance. But I could not call nor speak to anyone about it. There was nothing I could do and why would I fly to Panama and be stuck there with no hotel accommodations and have no idea how long it would take for me to get on another flight? I did pay for the insurance because I booked it far in advance and the flights were cheap. The only thing I could do was just wait until it was over and then book another flight.

So, Jeff left and was on his way. I ended up staying a whole another week in Peru by myself. The Airbnb guy was nice and let me move into another place he had. It was in the same building just on a different floor. However, trying to book another flight was horrible. As everyone was trying to get flights now. Plus, they were 10 times more expensive than when I first booked. I could not get a flight back to Tampa. The only one I could get was into Miami. Thankfully my husband is amazing and drove all the way down to get me.

Finally, I was back in Tampa safe and sound and I decided to submit my flights to the insurance I bought. But it was through some crappy company the airline had. What a nightmare. I fought with that insurance company for 6 months! Months of proving to them that a category 4 hurricane *actually* made landfall in Florida and that all airports were shut down and I couldn't board my flight. Like somehow, I faked 145 mph winds. That it was all fake news. Are you kidding me right now?! I compiled every newspaper article, information from the national hurricane center, actual screen shots from the Tampa Airport that they closed, and emails from the airline that they canceled my flights. After beating them over the head with real data they only refunded my initial flight of $250 but not the rebooked flight that was over $700 nor my extra Airbnb and food costs to stay in Peru. Total joke.

After that horrible experience we now use a private travel insurance company through one of my friends who is an agent. I will never buy travel insurance that is just "included" ever again. We use Chubbs which covers everything. It doesn't matter what happens or where you are, they will cover any travel delays, lost bags, medical, etc. And it's good for 1 calendar year. Then you just deal with the agent for claims. I think it's reasonable. If you travel a lot like we do, it's worth it to get good travel insurance. They have different level of plans that you can look into. Ours is around $400 per person. I read somewhere in the policy about loss of limbs. Hopefully that never happens, but you never know! One of my friends went cliff diving in Jamaica, she hit the water wrong and broke her back. She had to be life flighted back to Miami for emergency surgery. Then was in a back brace for months. I don't even want to know how much that costs.

Lesson is, get good insurance and be safe!

Chapter 15 Final Thoughts

Living in Peru for a month can be a rewarding and enriching experience, especially for digital nomads or slow travelers. The country offers visa-free entry for up to 90 days for many nationalities, making short-term stays simple and hassle-free. Peru is known for its affordability, with low costs for housing, food, and transportation, particularly outside of tourist-heavy areas. Cities like Lima, Arequipa, and Cusco offer decent infrastructure, coworking spaces, and reliable internet, making remote work feasible. The rich culture, world-class cuisine, and diverse landscapes—from mountains to beaches to deserts—make exploring Peru a real adventure. However, it's worth noting that there's no official digital nomad visa, and infrastructure in rural areas can be inconsistent. Adjusting to high altitudes and basic Spanish proficiency may also be necessary, but overall, Peru provides a vibrant and affordable base for a memorable month-long stay or even longer if you wish!

Use these tips in this book to help you along with your travels. As always, no matter where you go, always use your common sense as your guide. Travelers should use common sense because it helps them stay safe, respectful, and adaptable **in** unfamiliar environments. Using good judgment—like being aware of your surroundings, securing valuables, dressing appropriately, and avoiding risky behavior—can prevent theft, scams, or cultural misunderstandings. It also shows respect for local customs and people, which goes a long way in creating positive interactions. When you're navigating a new place, not everything goes as planned, so common sense helps you make smart decisions on the fly and respond calmly to unexpected situations. Basically, it's your best travel tool—free, reliable, and always with you.

Remember to have fun because at its core, travel is about joy, discovery, and creating memories. It's easy to get caught up in planning, logistics, or checking off bucket-list items—but the real magic happens when you let go a little and stay present. Having fun means embracing the unexpected, laughing at mishaps, trying weird foods, dancing to music you've never heard before, and connecting with people from all walks of life. Fun brings lightness to your journey and helps you truly experience the places you're visiting, not just pass through them. After all, these are the moments you ll look back on and smile about the most.

I wish you the best of luck in all your travels! Never stop exploring.

About the Author

Tara Richter-Hatzilias is the President of Richter Publishing LLC. She specializes in helping business owners how to write their non-fiction story in 4 weeks & publish a book in order to become an expert in their industry. She has been featured on CNN, ABC, Daytime TV, FOX, SSN, Channel 10 News, USA TODAY, Beverly Hills Times and radio stations all over the world.

Her degree is in Graphic Design and she worked in the copy and print industry in the Silicon Valley. She has written and published 15 of her own books in a span of about 10 years. Tara now has published many other authors all over the world including Anthony Amos & celebrity entrepreneur, Kevin Harrington, Shark from ABC's "Shark Tank" with their joint book, "How to Catch a Shark." She has also worked with many doctors, lawyers, non-profits and Fortune 500 Corporations such as Blooming Inc.

Tara has ventured to over 45 different countries from the time she was knee-high to a grasshopper, as her father would say. She has a passion for learning other cultures, eating exotic foods and meeting new people. She lives with her husband in Florida, but always planning their next adventure.

She can be reached on her website www.richterpublishing.com.

www.ingramcontent.com/pod-product-compliance
Lightning Source LLC
Chambersburg PA
CBHW071119090426
42736CB00012B/1954